QUOTATIONS FOR OCCASIONS

ELIZABETH KNOWLES

Quotations
for Occasions

Collins

HarperCollins Publishers
Westerhill Road
Bishopbriggs
Glasgow
G64 2QT

First edition 2008

Reprint 10 9 8 7 6 5 4 3 2 1 0

ISBN 978-0-00-726956-3

Collins® is a registered trademark of
HarperCollins Publishers Limited

www.collinslanguage.com

A catalogue record for this book is
available from the British Library

Designed by Mark Thomson

Typeset by Thomas Callan

Printed and bound in Italy by
LEGO Spa, Lavis (Trento), Italy

EDITORIAL STAFF
Ian Brookes
Lucy Cooper
Leonie Dunlop
Robert Groves
Helen Hucker
Cormac McKeown
Hannah Skehill

PUBLISHING DIRECTOR
Elaine Higgleton

Introduction

Expressions such as 'lost for words' and 'left speechless' illuminate a common problem: at a key moment we find ourselves searching for the right words. At such times it is natural to turn to others for help – and we often find that something said or written by another person at another time expresses exactly what we want to say. As Montaigne put it, 'I quote others ... the better to express myself.'

Quotations for Occasions offers a rich choice of quotations for use, across a range of subjects from **Achievement** ('I'm tired of dreaming. I'm into doing at the moment') to **Youth**. The focus on making the selection has been on the personal experience of people involved in a particular field. Topics covered range widely to include events of both personal and professional life. If you want to congratulate a friend on a new job or a promotion, you may find just what you are looking for under **Business** ('We were searching for employees and people turned up instead') or **Success**. The acquisition (or proud ownership) of a new pet might be marked by a comment under **Cats** ('One cat just leads to another') or **Dogs**. Leisure pursuits are covered by subject areas such as **Fishing** ('Transcendental meditation with a punchline') and **Gardens** ('The love of gardening is a seed that once sown never dies'). Sections such as **Love, Marriage** ('The heart of marriage is memories') and **Birth** touch on traditional happy events.

There are of course times also when there is need for

sympathy and consolation rather than rejoicing. The section on **Bereavement** offers both Iris Murdoch's evocation of 'a darkness impenetrable to the imagination of the un-bereaved', and C. S. Lewis's judgement that 'Bereavement is a universal and integral part of our experience of love.' Less seriously, someone who has problems with **Punctuality** may be encouraged by Marilyn Monroe's unworried, 'I've been on a calendar, but never on time.' (The difficulty, of course, can sometimes be attributed to the time chosen: according to Jean-Paul Sartre 'Three o'clock is always too late or too early for anything you want to do.')

For those who, contemplating **Birthdays**, feel that time is passing too quickly, there may be consolation in the philoso-phy of the astronaut John Glenn, that despite all the advanc-es in science and medicine 'There is no cure for the common birthday.' Bette Davis had a wry take on **Age**, cherishing a cushion with the embroidered maxim 'Old age ain't no place for sissies.' The former First Lady and diplomat Elean-or Roosevelt, however, resisted attempts to make her slow down: 'I could not, at any age, be really contented to take my place by the fireside and simply look on.' Someone contem-plating their **Appearance** might feel with Jean Cocteau that 'Mirrors should reflect a little before throwing back images.' They could however learn from Gloria Steinem's admirably confident response to a reporter who had said that she didn't look forty: 'This is what forty looks like.'

Topics which are of interest to us today inevitably bring together some very different perspectives. At **Nature** we have George Monbiot's observation that 'The middle classes think they have gone green because they have bought organic cotton pyjamas, and use hand-made soap with bits of leaf in it' and Jeremy Clarkson's somewhat startling assertion that 'There will be no leaf, tree, cloud, lawn, peat bog or environmental precious place that I won't drive over.' At **Diets**, Nigella Lawson's 'People don't have to be greedy, but it seems to me that life is a whole lot better if you enjoy food' contrasts with a simple statement attributed to the French novelist Colette: 'If I can't have too many truffles, I'll do without truffles.' Comments on **Food** include Jamie Oliver's regrets that 'Many kids can tell you about drugs but do not know what celery or courgettes taste like', and Sophia Loren's simple assertion 'All I am I owe to spaghetti.'

Quotations have largely been taken from what is being quoted today, and particular attention has been paid to those quotations which are quoted online. (We may think of ourselves as a cynical age, but the motivational and inspirational utterances of earlier years appear to be undergoing something of a refresher on personal websites.) However, having validated the selection overall by this identification of its base material, I have often made a final choice according to my own pleasure and interest.

As well as providing quotations for use, *Quotations for Occasions* offers opportunities for pleasurable browsing. Each subject area has an introductory section which surveys some of the main approaches to the area, and compares and contrasts the views of notable figures of past and present. A full index of authors provides biographical information about everyone who is quoted in the book, and a further index lists all of the main quotations alphabetically as an aid to retrieving a quotation whose subject is not known.

A generous level of cross-referencing allows you to find your way between related entries: at **Families**, for example, you will find references to **Children**, **Fathers**, **Mothers** ('There is nothing more thrilling in this world, I think, than having a child that is yours and yet is mysteriously a stranger'), and **Parents**. There is also a thematic index to guide you to the most appropriate section for your needs.

There is no end to what might be quoted, and there have of course been many dictionaries of quotations, as there are now many websites, offering lists of quotations on various subjects. This book's distinctive take is to focus its selection in accordance with personal experience, and to offer an overview of how a topic has struck people through the years, as well as how we may see it today. It has been enormously enjoyable to compile; I hope that it will offer readers a similar level of pleasure as well as usefulness.

Elizabeth Knowles
March 2008

* * *

Achievement

see also Careers, Success

'Just to stir things up seemed a great reward in itself', said the Roman historian Sallust, a sentiment which perhaps finds an echo in Arthur Hugh Clough's Victorian adjuration, 'Say not the struggle naught availeth.' The approach would not, however, find universal agreement: in the twentieth century, James Thurber commented acerbically, 'No man ... who has wrestled with a self-adjusting card table can ever be quite the same man he once was.' He might or might not have been able to subscribe to Winston Churchill's requirement (in rather more dramatic circumstances): 'Give us the tools, and we will finish the job.'

Achievement may be attributed to ability or effort. The painter Joshua Reynolds, while believing that innate ability was important, thought that it was not the whole story. 'If you have great talents, industry will improve them; if you have but moderate abilities, industry will supply their deficiencies.' He would have sympathized with the Russian ballerina Anna Pavlova, who said that 'Success depends in very large measure upon individual initiative and exertion, and cannot be achieved except by dint of hard work.' The French novelist Colette added another essential ingredient: to like what you are doing. 'One only does well what one loves doing. Neither science nor conscience makes a great cook. What use is application where inspiration is what's needed?'

In the end, however, some degree of talent is probably

an indispensable commodity for achievement. The Roman Emperor Galerius, addressing an archer who had consistently failed to hit a target, is said to have congratulated him sardonically: 'Not to have hit once in so many trials, argues the most splendid talents for missing.' As Elbert Hubbard said, 'One machine can do the work of fifty ordinary men. No machine can do the work of one extraordinary man.'

Miracles can be made, but only by sweating.
– Giovanni Agnelli

I'm tired of dreaming. I'm into doing at the moment.
– Bono

Fame is not achieved by sitting on feather cushions or lying in bed.
– Dante

It's the doing of it that's important. Not the measure. Not the measure. Not the measure. It's the doing.
– Betty Friedan

Everybody has talent, it's just a matter of moving around until you've discovered what it is.
– George Lucas

Ordinary people are capable of doing extraordinary things.
– Studs Terkel

Twenty years from now you will be more disappointed by the things you didn't do than by the ones you did do.
– MARK TWAIN

In Italy for thirty years under the Borgias they had warfare, terror, murder, bloodshed – they produced Michelangelo, Leonardo da Vinci and the Renaissance. In Switzerland they had brotherly love, five hundred years of democracy and peace, and what did they produce ...? The cuckoo clock.
– ORSON WELLES

* * *

Acting

see also Film

Despite his friendship for David Garrick, Samuel Johnson is on record with a characteristically caustic view of actors: 'Players, Sir! I look upon them as no better than creatures set upon tables and joint stools to make faces and produce laughter, like dancing dogs.' Across the centuries, he might have been sympathetic to the comment of the American actress and gossip columnist Hedda Hopper on a would-be fellow thespian: 'At one time I thought he wanted to be an actor. He had certain qualifications, including no money and a total lack of responsibility.' Marlon Brando suggested another drawback to theatrical society: 'An actor's a guy who, if you ain't talking about him, ain't listening.' Against this, however, we can set Elaine Dundy's comment on a particular difficulty for the actor: 'The question actors most often get asked is how they can bear saying the same things night after night, but God knows the answer to that is, don't we all anyway; might as well get paid for it.'

James Stewart thought that success was achieved if he could play a part 'and not have the acting show'. Occasionally, the effort made by an actor to get into the skin of the part has come in for criticism. The American critic George S. Kaufman said of Raymond Massey's portrayal of Abraham Lincoln: 'Massey won't be satisfied until somebody assassinates him.' And when Dustin Hoffman stayed up all night, in accordance with the experience of his character in the film *Marathon Man*, Laurence Olivier is reported to have asked, 'Why not try acting? It's much easier.'

Some famous theatrical quotations recall great figures of the past. Samuel Taylor Coleridge said of the tragic actor Edmund Kean, 'To see him act is like reading Shakespeare by flashes of lightning.' And one of Queen Victoria's ladies-in-waiting, privileged to see Sarah Bernhardt as Cleopatra, is said to have commented in a shocked voice, 'How different, how very different, from the home life of our own dear Queen!'

A painter paints, a musician plays, a writer writes – but a movie actor waits.

– MARY ASTOR

Acting is a form of confusion.
– TALLULAH BANKHEAD

Without wonder and insight, acting is just a trade. With it, it becomes creation.
– BETTE DAVIS

Actors don't pretend to be other people; they become themselves by finding other people inside them.
– DAVID MALOUF

The art of acting consists in keeping people from coughing.
– RALPH RICHARDSON

Rehearsing a play is making the word flesh. Publishing a play is reversing the process.
– PETER SHAFFER

Imagination! Imagination! I put it first years ago, when I was asked what qualities I thought necessary for success upon the stage.
– ELLEN TERRY

* * *

Advertising

see also **Business, Writing**

'Advertising', said the Canadian humorist Stephen Leacock, 'may be described as the science of arresting the human intelligence long enough to get money from it.' The American writer Zelda Fitzgerald sadly described the result that this had had for her: 'We grew up founding our dreams on the infinite promise of American advertising. I still believe that one can learn to play the piano by mail, and that mud will give you a perfect complexion.' She would presumably have agreed with Samuel Johnson's dictum that 'Promise, large promise, is the soul of an advertisement.' (Against this, the third President of the United States Thomas Jefferson thought that 'Advertisements contain the only truths to be relied on in a newspaper' – although it is not clear whether this comment said more about the advertisements or the newspaper.)

Most of these quotations focus on the effect that advertisements may have, but Aldous Huxley took another line. He was interested, not in the morality involved, but in the technical achievement. 'It is far easier to write ten passably effective sonnets, good enough to take in the not too inquiring critic, than one effective advertisement that will take in a few thousand of the uncritical buying public.' The English manufacturer and philanthropist Lord Leverhulme pointed wryly to another difficulty: 'Half the money I spend on advertising is wasted, and the trouble is I don't know which half.' However, he did not question its importance: as the American President Calvin Coolidge said in 1926, 'Advertising is the life of trade.'

An advertising agency is 85 per cent confusion and 15 per cent commission.
– FRED ALLEN

Let us prove to the world that good taste, good art, and good writing can be good selling.
– BILL BERNBACH

Advertising is the most fun you can have with your clothes on.
– JERRY DELLA FEMINA

Advertising, with its judicious mixture of flattery and threats.
– NORTHROP FRYE

The art of publicity is a black art, but it has come to stay.
– LEARNED HAND

Society drives people crazy with lust and calls it advertising.
– JOHN LAHR

Advertising is a valuable economic factor because it is the cheapest way of selling goods, particularly if the goods are worthless.
– SINCLAIR LEWIS

Ads are the cave art of the twentieth century.
– MARSHALL MCLUHAN

* * *

Advice

'Who cannot give good counsel? 'Tis cheap, it costs them nothing' said the seventeenth-century writer and clergyman Robert Burton, a sentiment echoed in his own time by the French moralist La Rochefoucauld: 'One gives nothing so generously as advice.' The readiness to offer advice was noted wryly centuries later by the American writer Annie Sullivan, famous as the teacher and companion of Helen Keller: 'It's queer how ready people always are with advice in any real or imaginary emergency, and no matter how many times experience has shown them to be wrong, they continue to set forth their opinions, as if they had received them from the Almighty!' Nor does it necessarily help if the person offering advice is speaking with special knowledge. According to the nineteenth-century Prime Minister Lord Salisbury: 'You should never trust experts. If you believe the doctors, nothing is wholesome: if you believe the theologians, nothing is innocent: if you believe the soldiers, nothing is safe. They all require to have their strong wine diluted by a very large admixture of insipid common sense.'

The picture here is that advice is often readily and rather thoughtlessly given, but Lord Chesterfield takes another perspective: 'Advice is seldom welcome; and those who want it the most, always like it the least.' The critic John Churton Collins had reservations about possible motives in seeking for advice: 'To ask advice is in nine cases out of ten to tout for flattery.'

I think I owe my success (as the millionaires say) to having listened respectfully and rather bashfully to the very best advice ... and then going away and doing the exact opposite.
– G. K. CHESTERTON

A word to the wise ain't necessary – it's the stupid ones who need the advice.
– BILL COSBY

Advice? I don't offer advice. Not my business. Your life is what you make it.
– BETTY FRIEDAN

Advice is what we ask for when we already know the answer but wish we didn't.
– ERICA JONG

No one wants advice, only corroboration.
– JOHN STEINBECK

I have lived some thirty years on this planet, and I have yet to hear the first syllable of valuable or even earnest advice from my seniors.
– HENRY DAVID THOREAU

I have found the best way to give advice to your children is to find out what they want and then advise them to do it.
– HARRY S TRUMAN

* * *

Age

see also Middle Age, Youth

Some reactions to old age can be decidedly negative. John Quincy Adams, sixth President of the United States, is said to have summed up the physical weakness associated with growing old in terms of a dilapidated building: 'I inhabit a weak, frail, decayed tenement; battered by the winds and broken in on by the storms, and, from all I can learn, the landlord does not intend to repair.' Presumably Adams resembled physically the man described by P. G. Wodehouse: 'He was either a man of about a hundred and fifty who was rather young for his years or a man of about a hundred and ten who had been aged by trouble.' The actress Bette Davis had a cushion embroidered with the words, 'Old age ain't no place for sissies.'

Consideration of one's own age can involve some level of denial. 'I still think of myself as I was twenty-five years ago,' said the comedian Dave Allen, adding 'Then I look in a mirror and see an old bastard and realize it's me.' The novelist Ivy Compton-Burnett is supposed to have said of someone claiming to be younger than she was: 'Pushing forty? She's clinging on to it for dear life.' The beautician Helena Rubinstein would probably have felt some sympathy for Dame Ivy's victim, but even she felt that all things must come to an end: 'I have always felt that a woman has a right to treat the subject of her age with ambiguity until, perhaps, she passes into the realm of over ninety. Then it is better she be candid with herself and with the world.'

Old age does have its own advantages. The American journalist and editor I. F. Stone was quoted in the 1970s as saying, 'If you live long enough, the venerability factor creeps in; you get accused of things you never did and praised for virtues you never had.' Perhaps anyone inclined to congratulate themselves on the praise should remember the sardonic verdict of Groucho Marx, quoted by Queen Elizabeth II at her eightieth birthday celebration: 'Anyone can get old. All you have to do is live long enough.' Or as Sophie Tucker said succinctly on the secret of longevity: 'Keep breathing.'

Age is strictly a case of mind over matter. If you don't mind, it doesn't matter
– JACK BENNY

Old age takes away from us what we have inherited and gives us what we have earned.
– GERALD BRENAN

We do not necessarily improve with age: for better or worse, we become more like ourselves.
– PETER HALL

When grace is joined with wrinkles, it is adorable. There is an unspeakable dawn in happy old age.
– VICTOR HUGO

I will not make age an issue of this campaign. I am not going to exploit for political purposes my opponent's youth and inexperience.
– RONALD REAGAN

I could not, at any age, be really contented to take my place by the fireside and simply look on.
– ELEANOR ROOSEVELT

Age is foolish and forgetful when it underestimates youth.
– J. K. ROWLING

There are compensations for growing older. One is the realization that to be sporting isn't at all necessary. It is a great relief to reach this stage.
– CORNELIA OTIS SKINNER

* * *

Ambition

see also Achievement, Careers, Work

'Ah, but a man's reach should exceed his grasp, Or what's a heaven for?' asked the painter Andrea del Sarto in Robert Browning's poem. A later artist has left an interesting record of the possible goals of such ambition. According to Salvador Dali: 'At the age of six I wanted to be a cook. At seven I wanted to be Napoleon. And my ambition has been growing steadily ever since.' In the film *Pretty Woman*, Julia Roberts as Vivian said simply, 'I want the fairy tale.'

The balance between ambition and realization has been taken up by the writer Louis de Bernières: 'The trouble with fulfilling your ambitions is you think you will be transformed into some sort of archangel and you're not. You still have to wash your socks.' Thomas Keneally, on the other hand, thought that conscious ambition did not necessarily result in achievement. 'It's only when you abandon your ambitions that they become possible.'

Ambition can be dangerous to its possessor. Shakespeare's Macbeth, steeling himself to the murder of Duncan, reflected on 'Vaulting ambition, which o'erleaps itself.' Joseph Conrad, however, took a measured view: 'All ambitions are lawful except those which climb upward on the miseries or credulities of mankind.'

Ambition in the working world is likely to be focused on the possibilities of promotion, although the American writer and historian Frank Moore Colby once wrote, 'I have found some of the best reasons I ever had for remaining at the bottom simply by looking at the men at the top.' He would have sympathized with the witches of Terry Pratchett's Discworld: 'Unlike wizards, who like nothing better than a complicated hierarchy, witches don't go in much for the structural approach to career progression.'

It is by attempting to reach the top at a single leap that so much misery is produced in the world.
– WILLIAM COBBETT

If you can dream it, you can do it.
– WALT DISNEY

Ambitious people climb, but faithful people build.
– JULIA WARD HOWE

I am ambitious. But if I weren't as talented as I am ambitious I would be a gross monstrosity.
– MADONNA

If you're going to be thinking anyway, you might as well think big.
– DONALD TRUMP

All my life I wanted to be someone. Now I see that I should have been more specific.
– JANE WAGNER

* * *

Appearance

see also Diets, Fashion

The nineteenth-century poet George Crabbe called the face 'the index of a feeling mind'. Whether or not everyone would agree with this, possession of a beautiful face has often been seen as a resource of great power. In the seventeenth century, Pascal thought that 'If Cleopatra's nose had been shorter the whole face of the earth would have changed.' Snow White's wicked stepmother was enraged to hear from her magic mirror that she was no longer 'the fairest in all the land'. (She would probably have agreed with Jean Cocteau's dry comment that 'Mirrors should reflect a little before throwing back images.')

The poet Thomas Campion wrote lyrically of a young woman, 'There is a garden in her face, Where roses and white lilies grow.' However, a perfect complexion may not last. The politician Nancy Astor refused firmly to pose for a photograph: 'Take a close-up of a woman past sixty! You might as well use a picture of a relief map of Ireland.' In our own time, Julie Burchill has commented, 'It has been said that a pretty face is a passport. But it's not, it's a visa, and it runs out fast.' Although there may be remedies for this: Helena Rubinstein thought that 'There are no ugly women, only lazy ones.'

Appearance, of course, is not dependent only on the face – nor are women the only ones to be concerned about how they may look. The American singer James Brown thought there were two essentials: 'Hair is the first thing. And teeth the second. Hair and teeth. A man got those two things he's got it all.' There is however consolation even for those who cannot meet James Brown's criteria. As Logan Pearsall Smith said reassuringly, 'There is more felicity on the other side of baldness than the young can possibly imagine.'

He might have brought an action for damages against his countenance, and won heavy damages.
– CHARLES DICKENS

There are two reasons why I'm in show business, and I'm standing on both of them.
– BETTY GRABLE

Beauty is handed out as undemocratically as inherited peerages, and beautiful people have done nothing to deserve their astonishing reward.
– JOHN MORTIMER

I'm not offended by dumb blonde jokes because I know I'm not dumb, and I know I'm not blonde.
– DOLLY PARTON

This is what forty looks like.
– GLORIA STEINEM
(on turning forty, to a reporter who had commented that she didn't look her age)

It is only shallow people who do not judge by appearances.
– OSCAR WILDE

One can never be too thin or too rich.
– DUCHESS OF WINDSOR

* * *

The Armed Forces

It was Dr Johnson's view that 'Every man thinks meanly of himself for not having been a soldier, or not having been at sea.' It is certainly true that, from Chaucer's 'parfit gentil knyght' on, literature is full of impressive images of military men. Shakespeare's Cleopatra, lamenting her lover Antony, saw him as a soldier: 'O, withered is the garland of the war, The soldier's pole is fallen!' With his death, 'there is nothing left remarkable Beneath the visiting moon.'

Antony was a Roman general, but there are some quotations which focus on the men to whom generals gave orders. Tennyson contributed a lasting phrase to the language when he wrote of the Charge of the Light Brigade, 'Theirs not to reason why.' The idea of a company destroyed because 'someone had blundered' was to be developed more keenly in the words of the First World War poet, Siegfried Sassoon. Harry and Jack, on their way up to the line, were greeted by a 'cheery old card' of a General who, as it turned out, 'did for them both by his plan of attack.' This is a bleak picture, but of course other comments celebrate a determination that was successful as well as heroic. Nelson, at the battle of Copenhagen in 1801, quite literally 'turned a blind eye' to the order to disengage. 'Leave off action? Now, damn me if I do! ... I have only one eye – I have a right to be blind sometimes.' 'Never in the field of human conflict was so much owed by so many to so few,' said Winston Churchill of the Battle of Britain pilots.

There are also other elements of military life that deserve consideration. Some are practical, along the lines of a saying attributed to the first Duke of Marlborough, 'No soldier can fight unless he is properly fed on beer and beef.' Others may touch on the motives through which someone has joined a particular service. Yeats's Irish airman, disclaiming the promptings of law, duty, or cheering crowds, attributed his choice to his desire for flight: 'A lonely impulse of delight Drove to this tumult in the clouds.'

The royal navy of England hath ever been its greatest defence and ornament; it is its ancient and natural strength; the floating bulwark of the island.
– WILLIAM BLACKSTONE

It is upon the Navy under the good providence of God that the safety, honour, and welfare of this realm do chiefly depend.
– CHARLES II

Oh, I have slipped the surly bonds of earth,
And danced the sky on laughter-silvered wings.
– JOHN GILLESPIE MAGEE

'A soldier's life is terrible hard,' says Alice.
– A. A. MILNE

The sailor tells stories of winds, the ploughman of bulls;
the soldier counts his wounds, the shepherd his sheep.
– PROPERTIUS

You can always tell an old soldier by the inside of his
holsters and cartridge boxes. The young ones carry
pistols and cartridges: the old ones, grub.
– GEORGE BERNARD SHAW

As Lord Chesterfield said of the generals of his day, 'I
only hope that when the enemy reads the list of their
names, he trembles as I do.'
– DUKE OF WELLINGTON

* * *

Arrival

see also Departure, Travel

Not all arrivals are welcome, or easy. In *A Midsummer Night's Dream*, the first encounter between Oberon and his estranged queen is marked by his greeting 'Ill met by moonlight, proud Titania.' The seventeenth-century preacher Lancelot Andrewes, reviewing the laborious journey of the Magi to Bethlehem, gave a vivid picture of what they had to go through: 'A cold coming they had of it, at this time of the year; just, the worst time of the year to take a journey, and specially a long journey, in. The ways deep, the weather sharp, the days short, the sun farthest off ... the very dead of winter.' In the world of Douglas Adams's *Hitch-Hiker's Guide to the Galaxy*, encounters may be regarded with considerable reserve. The gloomy robot Marvin negotiated a thicket of negatives to pronounce of Trillian, 'That young girl ... is one of the least benightedly unintelligent organic life forms it has been my profound lack of pleasure not to be able to avoid meeting.' This convoluted remark seems to conform to Elizabeth Bowen's view that 'Meeting people unlike oneself does not enlarge one's outlook; it only confirms one's idea that one is unique.'

The Magi at least would presumably have judged that what they found justified all the effort and discomfort, and hearteningly there are many voices to assert the exciting possibilities of an arrival, and a new encounter. Sometimes the promise is romantic, as in Oscar Hammerstein II's suggestion that 'Some enchanted evening, You may see a stranger, Across a crowded room.' The writer Anaïs Nin thought that 'Each friend represents a world in us, a world possibly not born until they arrive, and it is only by this meeting that a new world is born.'

The pain of parting is nothing to the joy of meeting again.
– CHARLES DICKENS

The meeting of two personalities is like the contact of two chemical substances: if there is any reaction, both are transformed.
– CARL JUNG

Ships that pass in the night, and speak each other in passing.
– HENRY WADSWORTH LONGFELLOW

Their meetings made December June.
– LORD TENNYSON

A star shines on the hour of our meeting.
– J. R. R. TOLKIEN

When two beings who are not friends are near one another there is no meeting; when they are at a distance, there is no separation.
– SIMONE WEIL

* * *

Art

see also **Criticism, Music**

'A picture,' said the nineteenth-century painter Samuel Palmer, 'has been said to be something between a thing and a thought.' Other artists of past and present have left comments on what they have achieved – and on what they were trying to do. Pablo Picasso said, 'Painting is a blind man's profession. He paints not what he sees, but what he feels.' Sometimes, of course, that can lead to difficulties. The famous portrait painter John Singer Sargent said ruefully, 'Every time I paint a portrait I lose a friend.'

The business approach to art has also been considered. The critic John Ruskin said magisterially of Whistler's paintings that he had 'never expected to hear a coxcomb ask two hundred guineas for flinging a pot of paint in the public's face.' (Whistler himself, when challenged as to his asking two hundred guineas for 'two days labour', replied, 'I ask it for the knowledge of a lifetime.') The Australian painter Sidney Robert Nolan commented, 'A successful artist would have no trouble being a successful member of the Mafia.' The famous American folk artist Anna Mary Moses, known as 'Grandma Moses', said, 'I don't advise anyone to take it up as a business proposition, unless they really have talent.'

Technique has also been a matter of interest. The painter John Opie, when asked how he mixed his colours, replied, 'I mix them with my brains.' In our own time, Damien Hirst commented, 'It's amazing what you can do with an E in A-level Art, twisted imagination, and a chainsaw.'

The sound of water escaping from mill-dams, etc., willows, old rotten planks, slimy posts, and brickwork, I love such things ... those scenes made me a painter and I am grateful.
– JOHN CONSTABLE

Drawing is the truest test of art.
– J. A. D. INGRES

I never painted dreams. I painted my own reality.
– FRIDA KAHLO

A picture never changed the price of eggs. But a picture can change our dreams; and pictures may in time clarify our values.
– ALLAN KAPROW

The painting has a life of its own. I try to let it come through.
– JACKSON POLLOCK

Skill without imagination is craftsmanship and gives us many useful objects such as wickerwork picnic baskets. Imagination without skill gives us modern art.
– TOM STOPPARD

If Botticelli were alive today he'd be working for *Vogue*.
– PETER USTINOV

* * *

23

Babies

see also Birth, Children, Families, Parents

Babies evoke a variety of reactions, from the warm to the detached. Jacques's 'seven ages of man' speech in Shakespeare's *As You Like It* marks the first age with the image of 'the infant Mewling and puking in the nurse's arms.' Wordsworth evoked the idea of the new-born infant arriving in this world 'trailing clouds of glory'. The ten-year-old Louisa May Alcott recorded in her diary her answer to her father's question as to 'God's noblest work': 'Anna said *men*, but I said *babies*. Men are often bad; babies never are.'

In the twentieth century, American humorist Leo Rosten, in a comment often attributed to W. C. Fields, said sweepingly, 'Any man who hates dogs and babies can't be all bad.' Against that, we have Winston Churchill's take on the economy: 'There is no finer investment for any community than putting milk into babies.'

The Princess Royal's attitude to pregnancy, perhaps unsurprisingly, puts her in the category of the detached. She said in an interview, 'It's a very boring time. I am not particularly maternal – it's an occupational hazard of being a wife.' The writer Kathy Lette said wryly, 'I used to rush to the mirror every morning to see if I had bloomed but all I did was swell. My ankles looked like flesh-coloured flares and my breasts were so huge they needed their own postcode.' She could of course have comforted herself with a comment from Peter Nicholls: '"One advantage of *being* pregnant," says a wife in one of my television plays, "you don't have to worry about *getting* pregnant.'" However, once the child has arrived, it will be welcomed. As Charles Dickens pointed out: 'It is a pleasant thing to reflect upon, and furnishes a complete answer to those who contend for the gradual degeneration of the human species, that every baby born into the world is a finer one than the last.'

The worst feature of a new baby is its mother's singing.
– KIN HUBBARD

If you desire to drain to the dregs the fullest cup of scorn and hatred a fellow human creature can pour out for you, let a young mother hear you call dear baby 'it'.
– JEROME K. JEROME

A loud noise at one end and no sense of responsibility at the other.
– RONALD KNOX

Loving a baby or child is a circular business, a kind of feedback loop.
– PENELOPE LEACH

No animal is so inexhaustible as an excited infant.
– AMY LESLIE

A baby is God's opinion that life should go on.
– CARL SANDBURG

A baby is an inestimable blessing and bother.
– MARK TWAIN

* * *

Belief

see also God

Belief has been seen as either an essential faculty, or a dangerous block on intellectual enquiry. 'Unless you believe, you will not understand,' said St Augustine. However, in the twentieth century the philosopher Bertrand Russell thought that 'Every man, wherever he goes, is encompassed by a cloud of comforting convictions, which move with him like flies on a summer day.' E. M. Forster reworked the biblical 'Lord, I believe; help thou mine unbelief' to 'Lord I disbelieve – help thou my unbelief.'

Systems of belief are not necessarily best explained by those who adhere to them. In Margot Asquith's Memoirs, she records the advice of the nineteenth-century scholar and Master of Balliol, Benjamin Jowett: 'My dear child, you must believe in God in spite of what the clergy tell you.' Lewis Carroll's Unicorn in Through the Looking-Glass suggested a bargain to Alice: 'If you'll believe in me, I'll believe in you.' Lord Melbourne, however, did not wish for any intervention in his personal beliefs. 'Things have come to a pretty pass when religion is allowed to invade the sphere of private life' was his reaction to hearing an evangelical sermon.

Julius Caesar thought that 'Men generally believe what they wish', and this links with a warning from John Henry Newman: 'We can believe what we choose. We are answerable for what we choose to believe.'

A belief is not true because it is useful.
– HENRI-FRÉDÉRIC AMIEL

I feel no need for any other faith than my faith in human beings.
– PEARL S. BUCK

There may be fairies at the bottom of the garden. There is no evidence for it, but you can't prove there aren't any, so shouldn't we be agnostic with respect to fairies?
– RICHARD DAWKINS

Reality is that which, when you stop believing it, doesn't go away.
– PHILIP K. DICK

As I get older I seem to believe less and less and yet to believe what I do believe more and more.
– DAVID JENKINS

One man's faith is another man's delusion.
– ANTHONY STORR

The courage to believe in nothing.
– IVAN TURGENEV

To believe in God is to yearn for his existence and, moreover, it is to behave as if he did exist.
– MIGUEL DE UNAMUNO

* * *

Bereavement

see also Death, Grief

Bereavement is a deeply personal experience of loss. In the biblical story, King David's response to the news of the death of his rebellious son Absalom culminated with the heartfelt wish, 'Would God I had died for thee, O Absalom, my son!'

In Shakespeare's *Macbeth*, the bereaved Macduff, hearing of the murder of his wife and children, is urged to 'Give sorrow words.' However, while speech may help the sufferer, it is not necessarily right for the person offering comfort. In 1853 Jane Welsh Carlyle wrote to her husband Thomas, after his mother had died, 'Never does one feel so helpless as in trying to speak comfort for a great bereavement. I will not try it.' At the beginning of the twentieth century, when a widow would naturally have gone into mourning clothes, George Bernard Shaw recommended a different way to a friend: 'Don't order any black things. Rejoice in his memory and be radiant: leave grief to the children. Wear violet and purple.'

For some, bereavement can (at least temporarily) block out all attempts to help. As Iris Murdoch wrote, 'Bereavement is a darkness impenetrable to the imagination of the unbereaved.' But the French airman Antoine de Saint-Exupéry offered a comfort beyond the immediate pain of loss when he wrote, 'For he who has gone, so we but cherish his memory, abides with us, more potent, nay, more present, than the living man.'

No other sun has lightened up my heaven,
No other star has ever shone for me.
– EMILY BRONTË

To live in hearts we leave behind
Is not to die.
– THOMAS CAMPBELL

Bereavement is a universal and integral part of our
experience of love.
– C. S. LEWIS

One must not let oneself be overwhelmed by sadness.
– JACQUELINE KENNEDY ONASSIS

I cannot forgive my friends for dying; I do not find these
vanishing acts at all amusing.
– LOGAN PEARSALL SMITH

On the death of a friend, we should consider that the fates through confidence have devolved on us the task of a double living, that we have henceforth to fulfil the promise of our friend's life also, in our own, to the world.
– HENRY DAVID THOREAU

* * *

Birth

see also Babies, Birthdays

Sigmund Freud thought that for the child, 'The act of birth is the first experience of anxiety.' It would certainly be reasonable to feel that this would have been true for Glendower in Shakespeare's *Henry IV Part 1*. By his own account, not only were the skies full of 'fiery shapes', but 'The frame and huge foundation of the earth Shaked like a coward.' (It is only fair to note that Hotspur, unimpressed by this picture, pointed out that the same phenomena would have been noted 'at the same season if your mother's cat had but kittened'.)

'My mother groaned! My father wept, Into the dangerous world I leapt,' wrote William Blake, and others have focused on the immediate circumstances of their birth. According to one of Congreve's characters, 'I came upstairs into the world; for I was born in a cellar.'

'Easier than having a tattoo', said Nicole Appleton, of childbirth from the mother's point of view, but others have been less dismissive. Queen Victoria, a mother of nine, responded sceptically to her eldest daughter, the Crown Princess of Prussia, when the Princess was expecting her first child. 'What you say of the pride of giving life to an immortal soul is very fine, dear, but I own I cannot enter into that; I think much more of our being like a cow or a dog at such moments; when our poor nature becomes so very animal and unecstatic.' J. K. Rowling cited it as an example of considerable, if temporary, pain to the mother: 'Poverty is a lot like childbirth – you know it's going to hurt before it happens, but you'll never know how much until you've experienced it.'

Unto us a child is born.
– THE BIBLE

I was born at the age of twelve on a Metro-Goldwyn-Meyer lot.
– JUDY GARLAND

I'm not interested in being Wonder Woman in the delivery room. Give me drugs.
– MADONNA

I think, at a child's birth, if a mother could ask a fairy godmother to endow it with the most useful gift, that gift should be curiosity.
– ELEANOR ROOSEVELT

There was a star danced, and under that was I born.
– WILLIAM SHAKESPEARE
(Beatrice's account of her birth in Much Ado About Nothing)

Our birth is but a sleep and a forgetting.
– WILLIAM WORDSWORTH

* * *

Birthdays

see also Age, Birth

Birthdays are traditionally a time of celebration, although it is possible that not everyone can achieve the tranquillity envisioned by Alexander Pope in the couplet, 'Pleased to look forward, pleased to look behind, And count each birthday with a grateful mind.' The American poet Robert Frost is said to have defined a diplomat as 'a man who always remembers a woman's birthday but never remembers her age'. This approach would have been appreciated by Dornford Yates's character Daphne Pleydell, who explained to a new friend that she was now counting backwards. 'Last year I was twenty-seven, so this year I am twenty-six. Entirely between ourselves, the Bilberry register will tell you I'm thirty-two.' She was improving on a principle stated by Oscar Wilde's Lady Bracknell: 'Thirty-five is a very attractive age. London society is full of women of the very highest birth who have, of their own free choice, remained thirty-five for years.'

Thomas Jefferson took an austere view, writing to a friend of his disapproval of 'transferring the honors and veneration for the great birthday of our Republic to any individual'. To ensure that this did not happen, 'I have declined letting my own birthday be known, and have engaged my family not to communicate it.' And Lewis Carroll's Humpty Dumpty pointed out to Alice another disadvantage of annual celebration: 'There are three hundred and sixty four days when you might get un-birthday presents ... and only one for birthday presents.'

I was born in 1896, and my parents were married in 1919.
– J. R. ACKERLEY

The worst gift is a fruitcake. There is only one fruitcake in the entire world, and people keep sending it to each other.
– JOHNNY CARSON

For all the advances in science and medicine ... one immutable fact remains. There is no cure for the common birthday.
– JOHN GLENN

The return of my birthday, if I remember it, fills me with thoughts which it seems to be the general care of humanity to escape.
– SAMUEL JOHNSON

It's my birthday today and I'd like you all to help me celebrate it.
– PLAUTUS

Our birthdays are feathers in the broad wing of time.
– JEAN PAUL RICHTER

* * *

Boats

see also Armed Forces, Travel

Quotations about ships and boats often evoke a picture of a particular vessel, from the romance and dignity of John Masefield's 'Quinquireme of Nineveh from distant Ophir', with its cargo of 'ivory, And apes and peacocks' to the 'beautiful pea-green boat' in which Edward Lear's Owl and Pussycat 'sailed away For a year and a day'. Boats have inspired a range of similes, from James Elroy Flecker's 'I have seen old ships sail like swans asleep Beyond that village which men still call Tyre', to Lord Byron's famous description of a gondola as 'a coffin clapt in a canoe'.

Ships have been associated with a moment of history. The escape of Charles Edward Stuart, the 'lad ... born to be a king', from the English soldiery, is commemorated by the Skye Boat Song, and its opening words, 'Speed, bonny boat, like a bird on the wing.' Two centuries later, Philip Guedalla wrote of the evacuation of Dunkirk, 'The little ships, the unforgotten

Homeric catalogue of Mary Jane and Peggy IV, of Folkestone Belle, Boy Billy, and Ethel Maud, of Lady Haig and Skylark ... the little ships of England brought the Army home.'

For some, life on board ship has offered all the education they have known. 'A whale ship was my Yale College and my Harvard,' said the narrator in Herman Melville's *Moby Dick*. For others, whether or not they are experiencing William Johnson Cory's 'Jolly boating weather', to be afloat is simply the way they would choose to spend their time. However, there may be disappointments. Irving Berlin's sailors in *Follow the Fleet* had 'joined the Navy to see the world', but in the end had a rather more limited experience: 'And what did we see? We saw the sea.'

They that go down to the sea in ships ... These see the works of the Lord.
– THE BIBLE

My boat is on the shore,
And my bark is on the sea.
– LORD BYRON

There is nothing – absolutely nothing – half so much worth doing as simply messing about in boats.
– KENNETH GRAHAME
(said by Water Rat to Mole in *The Wind in the Willows*)

A little stream best fits a little boat.
– ROBERT HERRICK

When you spend so much time pushing, caring for, cajoling and maintaining a beautiful racing machine like this, you get very close. She's looked after me well, and I look after her.
– Ellen MacArthur

All I ask is a tall ship and a star to steer her by.
– John Masefield

* * *

Boredom

see also Patience, Retirement

Lord Byron suggested that the 'polished horde' of Society could be divided into 'two mighty tribes, the Bores and the Bored'. Dylan Thomas, however, apparently once managed to combine the two factions. He had been talking copiously, but now he broke off. 'Somebody's boring me,' he said. 'I think it's me.'

There are various views of what makes a bore. Ambrose Bierce defined a bore as 'A person who talks when you wish him to listen'. The American journalist Bert Leston Taylor said that 'A bore is a man who, when you ask him how he is, tells you.' John Updike's calculation of the result was that 'A healthy male adult bore consumes one and a half times his own weight in other people's patience.' The first President George Bush, however, spoke up for those who do not attract or interest others: 'What's wrong with being a boring kind of guy?'

In all these assessments, the bored person is the blameless victim of the bore. G. K. Chesterton, however, suggested that part of the problem might lie with the listener: 'There is no such thing on earth as an uninteresting subject; the only thing that can exist is an uninterested person.'

Whatever the cause of boredom, there is consensus that the state is not a pleasing one. The clergyman Dean Inge, indeed, saw it as positively dangerous: 'The effect of boredom on a large scale in history is underestimated. It is a main cause of revolutions, and would soon bring to an end all the static Utopias and the farmyard civilization of the Fabians.' Bertrand Russell wrote that it was 'a vital problem for the moralist, since at least half the sins of mankind are caused by the fear of it'. And in the series of books for children by the American writer Kay Thompson about Eloise, a type of the 'poor little rich girl', who lives (and runs riot) in the Plaza Hotel, New York, we find Eloise's simple mantra 'Getting bored is not allowed.'

The penalty of success is to be bored by people who used to snub you.
– NANCY ASTOR

I mused for a few moments on the question of which was worse, to lead a life so boring that you are easily enchanted or a life so full of stimulus that you are easily bored.
– BILL BRYSON

Is ditchwater dull? Naturalists have told me it teems with quiet fun.
– G. K. CHESTERTON

If you resolve to give up smoking and drinking and loving, you don't actually live longer; it just seems longer.
– CLEMENT FREUD

The nice thing about being a celebrity is that, if you bore people, they think it is their fault.
– HENRY KISSINGER

Boredom is just the reverse side of fascination: both depend on being outside rather than inside a situation, and one leads to the other.
– SUSAN SONTAG

The secret of being boring is to say everything.
– VOLTAIRE

* * *

Bureaucracy

see also Business, Management, Meetings

Despite the persuasion of the Labour politician Douglas Jay (speaking in the idiom of his times) that 'the gentleman in Whitehall really does know best', bureaucracy does not have a good name for creativity or innovation. One unidentified speaker has defined a committee as 'a cul-de-sac down which ideas are lured and then quietly strangled'. Far from seeing safety in numbers, the actor Herbert Beerbohm Tree thought that 'A committee should consist of three men, two of whom are absent.' The American humorist Fred Allen saw a conference as 'a gathering of important people who singly can do nothing, but together can decide that nothing can be done'.

Sometimes a decision of this kind is self-protective; as the American statesman Dean Acheson reminded us, 'A memorandum is written not to inform the reader but to protect the writer.' Long before him, Charles Dickens had described the workings of the Circumlocution Office: 'Whatever was required to be done, the Circumlocution Office was beforehand with all the public departments in the art of perceiving – HOW NOT TO DO IT.' At other times, however, the failure to achieve anything of note in the corridors of power may be inadvertent. According to George Santayana, 'The working of great institutions is mainly the result of a vast mass of routine, petty malice, self interest, carelessness, and sheer mistake. Only a residual fraction is thought.'

Committee – a group of men who keep minutes and waste hours.
– MILTON BERLE

You can run the office without a boss, but you can't run an office without the secretaries.
– JANE FONDA

A Royal Commission is a broody hen sitting on a china egg.
– MICHAEL FOOT

Away with systems!
– GEORGE MEREDITH

Bureaucracy defends the status quo long past the time when the quo has lost its status.
– LAURENCE J. PETER

A difficulty for every solution.
– LORD SAMUEL
(of the civil service)

* * *

Business

see also Bureaucracy, Management, Opportunity, Success

The business world is not always associated with ethical practice. According to the economist Thorstein Veblen, 'All business sagacity reduces itself in the last analysis to the judicious use of sabotage.' Mario Puzo's Godfather, applying irresistible pressure, said ominously, 'He's a businessman. I'll make him an offer he can't refuse.' Even the law may not be a complete safeguard. The American bishop and broadcaster J. Fulton Sheen, considering his contract for a television appearance, warned, 'The big print giveth and the fine print taketh away.' According to the American civil rights campaigner Andrew Young's rueful assessment, 'Nothing is illegal if one hundred businessmen decide to do it.'

There are, of course, some positive things to be said. As a character in Jane Austen's *Emma* pointed out, 'Business, you know, may bring money, but friendship hardly ever does.' This sense of a strictly limited approbation can be found in other voices. Mahatma Gandhi thought that it was 'difficult but not impossible to conduct strictly honest business. What is true is that honesty is incompatible with the amassing of a large fortune'. (He would certainly have agreed with the comment of the American businessman and philanthropist Andrew Carnegie, considering the position of a person who has not used their surplus wealth to help others, 'The man who dies thus rich dies disgraced.')

'Business' in a wider sense is often seen as the opposite of 'pleasure', as in the assessment by the constitutionalist Walter Bagehot: 'Business is really more agreeable than pleasure. It interests the whole mind, the aggregate nature of man more continuously, and more deeply. But it does not look as if it did.' Nearer our own time, and looking at the business world of today, Donald Trump has said, 'Deals are my art form. Other people paint beautifully on canvas, or write wonderful poetry. I like making deals, preferably big deals. That's how I get my kicks.' This sentiment finds an echo in the words of Andy Warhol: 'Being good in business is the most fascinating kind of art.'

Be fearful when others are greedy and greedy only when others are fearful.
– WARREN BUFFETT

Here's the rule for bargains. 'Do other men, for they would do you.' That's the true business precept. All others are counterfeit.
– CHARLES DICKENS

The meek shall inherit the earth, but not the mineral rights.
– JOHN PAUL GETTY

The secret of business is to know something that nobody else knows.
– ARISTOTLE ONASSIS

In the factory we make cosmetics. In the store we sell hope.
– CHARLES REVSON

We were searching for employees and people turned up instead.
– ANITA RODDICK

It is difficult to get a man to understand something when his salary depends on his not understanding it.
– UPTON SINCLAIR

There's nothing wrong with being greedy, if you're a businessman, that's what it's about.
– ALAN SUGAR

*   *   *

Careers

see also Achievement, Ambition, Business, Management

For the upwardly mobile, a verse in the Bible offers the rather disheartening view that 'Promotion cometh neither from the east, nor from the west, nor from the south', and the question of how best to advance your own interests has been considered over many centuries. Such advance may of course bring more than one kind of risk: Francis Bacon wrote in the seventeenth century that 'All rising to great place is by a winding stair.' And success may breed resentment: the Sun King, Louis XIV of France, is reported as saying, 'Every time I make an appointment, I make a hundred men discontented and one ungrateful.' Self-interest is likely to colour your approach: as Harry Truman said, 'It's a recession when your neighbour loses his job; it's a depression when you lose your own.'

It was in the 1930s that the American lecturer and public speaker Dale Carnegie published his book *How to Win Friends and Influence People*, and thus added a phrase to the language. However, there has never been any shortage of advice for those wanting to follow what George Bernard Shaw called

43

'The Gospel of Getting On'. Sometimes, whether you have what are seen as the key qualities may be a matter of luck: Joan Bakewell in the 1990s observed that 'The BBC is full of men appointing men who remind them of themselves when young.'

There is also the possibility of good fortune in timing. In October 2007, reporting on the death of the writer and broadcaster Ned Sherrin, *The Times* quoted from his autobiography: 'In a long career of happy accidents, perhaps the most useful was to have been born in 1931 and to complete National Service, Oxford and bar exams precisely in time for the opening of commercial television.'

His was the sort of career that made the Recording Angel think seriously about taking up shorthand.
– NICOLAS BENTLEY

To do nothing and get something, formed a boy's ideal of a manly career.
– BENJAMIN DISRAELI

In a hierarchy every employee tends to rise to his level of incompetence.
– LAURENCE J. PETER

A life spent in constant labour is a life wasted, save a man be such a fool as to regard a fulsome obituary notice as ample reward.
– GEORGE JEAN NATHAN

You will find as you grow older that the weight of rages will press harder and harder upon the employer.
– WILLIAM SPOONER

The best careers advice to give to the young is 'Find out what you like doing best and get someone to pay you for doing it.'
– KATHARINE WHITEHORN

* * *

Cars

see also Progress, Travel

Since Henry Ford decreed that customers for the Model T Ford could have it in 'Any colour – so long as it's black', comments on cars have often evoked the look of a particular vehicle. The American poet Robert Lowell wrote in the 1960s that 'Giant finned cars nose forward like fish.' Barry Humphries in the persona of Dame Edna Everage greeted a Morris Traveller seen in Stratford-upon-Avon with the comment, 'Why, even the cars are half-timbered here!' Perhaps most strikingly, Lord Nuffield is supposed to have said in alarm, on seeing the prototype of the Mini, 'It looks like a poached egg.'

The verb 'to motor' was coined in 1895. Its use was proposed in a letter to the periodical *The Autocar* in December 1895, and the letter-writer added reflectively that 'It might strike us as rather funny now, if we read in the paper "Lord Salisbury motored" this afternoon from Downing Street, and arrived at Paddington Station at exactly six o'clock.' The leisured days of 'motoring' were left behind as the car increasingly became a natural part of life. In the 1960s, the American humorist Art Buchwald claimed: 'Americans are broad-minded people. They'll accept the fact that a person can be an alcoholic, a dope fiend, a wife beater, and even a newspaperman, but if a man doesn't drive, there is something wrong with him.' And for some drivers, the siren call of Kenneth Grahame's Mr Toad from *The Wind in the Willows* is all too clear: 'The real way to travel! Here today – in next week tomorrow! Villages skipped, towns and cities jumped – always somebody else's horizon! O bliss! O poop-poop! O my! O my!'

To argue that a car is simply a means of conveyance is like arguing that Blenheim Palace is simply a house
– JEREMY CLARKSON

Our motor car is our supreme form of privacy when away from home.
– MARSHALL MCLUHAN

Restore human legs as a means of travel. Pedestrians rely on food for fuel and need no special parking facilities.
– LEWIS MUMFORD

A world designed for automobiles instead of people would have wider streets, larger dining rooms, fewer stairs to climb and no smelly, dangerous subway stations.
– P. J. O'ROURKE

No other man-made device since the shields and lances of the ancient knights fulfils a man's ego like the automobile.
– LORD ROOTES

Everything in life is somewhere else, and you get there in a car.
– E. B. WHITE

* * *

Cats

see also Dogs

Cats in proverbs are seen as independent and self-sufficient creatures – 'a cat may look at a king', or 'a cat has nine lives.' In Kipling's *Just-So Stories*, the cat who 'walks by his wild lone' asserts: 'I am the Cat who walks by himself, and all places are alike to me.' Such animals are not readily impressed by humans, but may have particular views on how their own humans should behave. The religious writer Evelyn Underhill once told a friend, 'I have just been given a very engaging Persian kitten, named after St Philip Neri (who was very sound on cats) and his opinion is that I have been given to him.'

James Boswell told an anecdote about Dr Johnson's cat Hodge, which brings that creature vividly to life. According to this account, Boswell had commented to his friend that Hodge was a fine cat, to which the great lexicographer gave a qualified assent: 'Why yes, Sir, but I have had cats whom I liked better than this.' He presumably then became aware of a baleful look from his pet, as Boswell went on to tell us that, 'as if perceiving Hodge to be out of countenance', he added 'but he is very fine cat, a very fine cat indeed'. We are not told how Hodge received this belated attempt to curry favour.

Even the rather alarming Hodge must once have been a kitten – often taken as a type of the pretty and amusing: since the beginning of the twentieth century, 'a basket of kittens' has been used as a figure of speech to evoke the cosy or mischievous. The American writer Henry David Thoreau has given a clear picture of a kitten at its most endearing stage: 'A kitten is so flexible that she is almost double; the hind parts are equivalent to another kitten with which the forepart plays. She does not discover that her tail belongs to her until you tread on it.' But as the poet Ogden Nash has pointed out, the drawback of a kitten is that 'Eventually it becomes a cat.'

Authors like cats because they are such quiet, lovable, wise creatures, and cats like authors for the same reason.
– ROBERTSON DAVIES

There are eleven cats here. One cat just leads to another.
– ERNEST HEMINGWAY

I have noticed that what cats most appreciate in a human
being is not the ability to produce food – which they take
for granted – but his or her entertainment value.
– GEOFFREY HOUSEHOLD

If a fish is the movement of water embodied, given shape,
then a cat is a diagram and pattern of subtle air.
– DORIS LESSING

When I play with my cat, who knows whether she isn't
amusing herself with me more than I am with her?
– MICHEL DE MONTAIGNE

The playful kitten, with its pretty little tigerish gambols,
is infinitely more amusing than half the people one is
obliged to live with.
– SYDNEY MORGAN

Cats, no less liquid than their shadows,
Offer no angles to the wind.
– A. S. J. TESSIMOND

* * *

Celebrity

see also Success

'Fame is the spur that the clear spirit doth raise,' wrote John Milton in the seventeenth century. A famous person may become an iconic figure; when Abraham Lincoln was assassinated, Edwin McMasters Stanton, who had been Lincoln's Secretary of War, commented, 'Now he belongs to the ages.'

We may think of 'celebrity', as opposed to 'fame', as being a modern invention, but there have always been sudden superstars. Byron's *Childe Harolde's Pilgrimage*, published in 1812, sold out in three days. As the poet himself put it, 'I awoke one morning and found myself famous.'

The nineteenth-century actor Herbert Beerhohm Tree enjoyed his public profile, saying: 'When I pass my name in such large letters I blush, but at the same time I instinctively raise my hat.' Some later views of celebrity were less enthusiastic. The American critic H. L. Mencken wrote that 'A celebrity is one who is known to many persons he is glad he doesn't know.' And Walt Disney, at the height of his fame, was wryly aware of the limitations of being a household name: 'Being a celebrity has never helped me make a better picture ... It doesn't even seem to help keep the fleas off our dogs, and if being a celebrity won't even give you an advantage over a couple of fleas, then I guess there can't be much in being a celebrity after all!'

A celebrity is a person who works hard all his life to become known, then wears dark glasses to avoid being recognized.
– FRED ALLEN

Passion for fame; a passion that is the instinct of all great souls.
– EDMUND BURKE

I don't care what is written about me as long as it isn't true.
– KATHARINE HEPBURN

The best fame is a writer's fame: it's enough to get a table at a good restaurant, but not enough that you get interrupted when you eat.
– FRAN LEBOWITZ

If you have to tell them who you are, you aren't anybody.
– GREGORY PECK
(on not being recognized in a crowded restaurant)

The desire for fame is the last thing to be put aside, even by the wise.
– TACITUS

In the future everyone will be world famous for fifteen minutes.
– ANDY WARHOL

* * *

Change

see also **Progress, Technology**

The prospect of change is often viewed with some alarm. The nineteenth-century judge Sir John Astbury is supposed to have exclaimed, 'Reform! Reform! Aren't things bad enough already?' He might well have thought that change once introduced would be difficult to stop; as Machiavelli had written in the sixteenth century, 'One change always leaves the way prepared for the introduction of another.'

Proverbially, we are told that 'A change is as good as a rest.' While not everyone would feel able to agree with this, the American writer Washington Irving offered encouragement for those who are unable to subscribe to this idea: 'There is a certain relief in change, even though it be from bad to worse; as I have found in travelling in a stage-coach, that it is often a comfort to shift one's position and be bruised in a new place.' Or as Dr Johnson said, summarizing the view of the sixteenth-century theologian Richard Hooker, 'Change is not made without inconvenience, even from worse to better.'

The notion that change can be painful has been reinforced in our own time by Rupert Murdoch: 'I'm a catalyst for change. You can't be an outsider and be successful over thirty years without leaving a certain amount of scar tissue around the place.' However, despite the consensus (since classical times) that change is in the end unavoidable, we need not think of ourselves as helpless victims. A management slogan of the late 1990s held that 'Change imposed is change opposed', and a number of speakers from Mahatma Gandhi to Andy Warhol speak to the requirement for us to make changes for ourselves. And even where it is accepted that change is desirable, the person calling for it needs to take care. Barack Obama, campaigning for the Democratic presidential nomination in January 2008, told an audience ruefully, 'I've been campaigning a lot because today I said, "The time for come has changed."'

The universe is change; life is what thinking makes of it.
– MARCUS AURELIUS

They must often change who would be constant in happiness and wisdom.
– CONFUCIUS

Change is inevitable. In a progressive country, change is constant.
– BENJAMIN DISRAELI

We must be the change we hope to see in the world.
– MAHATMA GANDHI

Everything is on the move, nothing is constant.
– HERACLITUS

There is nothing like returning to a place that remains unchanged to find the ways you yourself have altered.
– NELSON MANDELA

Things do not change; we change.
– HENRY DAVID THOREAU

They always say time changes things, but you actually have to change them yourself.
– ANDY WARHOL

* * *

Children

see also Babies, Families, Parents

A number of quotations about children suggest that they may be regarded by the adult world with resignation rather than enthusiasm – although not everyone would go as far as Kingsley Amis in remarking that 'It was no wonder that people were so horrible when they started life as children.' Nor does there seem much hope that the raw material can be changed: in the 1920s, Dean Inge thought that 'The proper time to influence the character of a child is about a hundred years before he is born.' This is a comment that gives an interesting perspective on Wordsworth's view that 'The child is father of the man.'

Children may have their uses. In *Sense and Sensibility*, describing a visit made to Mrs Dashwood and her daughters by Sir John and Lady Middleton, Jane Austen applauded Lady Middleton's forethought in bringing her small son with her.

'On every formal visit a child ought to be of the party, by way of provision for discourse.'

There are, of course, affectionate quotations about children. In the seventeenth century, the English poet and clergyman Robert Herrick wrote a verse about a child at prayer which began, 'Here a little child I stand, Heaving up my either hand' – although the hands in question were 'cold as paddocks' (toads). But in the majority of cases the note is one of reservation, even if not everyone would wish to follow Gore Vidal's sardonic advice, 'Never have children, only grandchildren.'

Animals are always loyal and love you, whereas with children you never know where you are.
– CHRISTINA FOYLE

Having one child makes you a parent; having two you are a referee.
– DAVID FROST

I love children – especially when they cry, for then someone takes them away.
– NANCY MITFORD

One stops being a child when one realizes that telling one's trouble does not make it better.
– CESARE PAVESE

Parents learn a lot from their children about coping with life.
– MURIEL SPARK

There are only two things a child will share willingly – communicable diseases and his mother's age.
– BENJAMIN SPOCK

* * *

Chocolate

see also Diets, Food

G. K. Chesterton, a beer-drinker, considered that 'Cocoa is a cad and coward, Cocoa is a vulgar beast', but for many, chocolate in all its variations offers a very special experience. In the seventeenth century, the letter-writer Madame de Sévigné developed a (short-lived) passion for drinking chocolate. At the height of her enthusiasm, she told her daughter, 'If you are not feeling well, if you have not slept, chocolate will revive you.' In the nineteenth century, Laura Troubridge left details of the particular kind of chocolate she favoured, adding disarmingly, 'It is the only thing, except other sorts of choc. and ices, that I really *enjoy* eating.'

Thomas Jefferson, at the end of the eighteenth century, gave a positive if more measured judgement. Writing to John Adams in November 1785, he predicted that 'The superiority of the article [chocolate], both for health and nourishment, will soon give it the same preference over tea and coffee in America, which it has in Spain.' His prediction seems to be born out by the comment attributed to Milton Hershey, on selling his Lancaster Caramel Company in 1900, 'Caramels are just a fad, but chocolate is a permanent thing.' And from the world of Charles M. Schultz's *Peanuts*, it is widely quoted as Lucy's view that 'All I really need is love, but a little chocolate now and then doesn't hurt.'

Anything's good if it's made of chocolate.
– JO BRAND

I think the answer lies somewhere between conversation and chocolate.
– MEL GIBSON
(promoting his film *What Women Want*)

My momma always said life was like a box of chocolates ... you never know what you're gonna get.
– ERIC ROTH
(from the screenplay for the 1994 film *Forrest Gump*, spoken
 by the title character)

What use are cartridges in battle? I always carry chocolate instead.
– GEORGE BERNARD SHAW
(the military practice of the 'Chocolate Cream Soldier' in
 Arms and the Man)

Chocolate is not what it was to me. I was carried away by the fashion, as usual.
– MADAME DE SÉVIGNÉ

Plenty of chocolates with that goo-ey, slithery stuff in the middle.
– P. G. WODEHOUSE

* * *

Christmas

Many quotations associated with Christmas evoke familiar images. Carols give us the stable at Bethlehem, shepherds, angels, and the magi following a star. Secular songs add jingling sleigh bells, reindeer, holly and mistletoe.

The weather has long been of abiding interest. Centuries before Irving Berlin's 'I'm dreaming of a white Christmas', Thomas Fuller warned that 'A green Christmas is neither handsome nor healthful.' (He would presumably have been alarmed by Marcus Clarke's evocative account of Christmas in nineteenth-century Australia, 'A very merry Christmas, with roast beef in a violent perspiration, and the thermometer 110° in the shade!') In the eighteenth century, Joseph Addison's Sir Roger de Coverley said judicially that he had often thought that 'it happens very well that Christmas should fall out in the Middle of Winter'.

'Yes, Virginia, there is a Santa Claus' wrote the American journalist Francis P. Church in 1897, in a famous editorial in the New York *Sun* entitled 'Is There a Santa Claus?' (The eight-year-old Virginia O'Hanlon had written to the paper, 'Papa says "If you see it in *The Sun* it's so." Please tell me the truth; is there a Santa Claus?') Virginia's experience differed notably from that of the young Shirley Temple. In later life, she recalled the height of her fame as a child-star: 'I stopped believing in Santa Claus when I was six. Mother took me to see him in a department store, and he asked for my autograph.'

The poet John Betjeman wrote of a day when 'girls in slacks remember Dad, and oafish louts remember Mum', but many comments on Christmas focus on more self-indulgent aspects of the day. The nineteenth-century essayist and poet Leigh Hunt invoked Christmas with the words, 'Glorious time of great Too-Much'.

Christmas, children, is not a date. It is a state of mind.
– MARY ELLEN CHASE

I do like Christmas on the whole ... In its clumsy way, it does approach Peace and Goodwill.
– E. M. FORSTER

Christmas to a child is the first terrible proof that to travel hopefully is better than to arrive.
– STEPHEN FRY

The magi, as you know, were wise men ... They invented the art of giving Christmas presents.
– O. HENRY

The only real blind person at Christmas-time is he who has not Christmas in his heart.
– HELEN KELLER

To perceive Christmas through its wrapping becomes more difficult every year.
– E. B. WHITE

* * *

Communication

see also Conversation, Cyberspace

The seventeenth-century dramatist Aphra Behn said simply, 'Money speaks sense in a language all nations understand.' Beyond this reduction to essentials, we communicate in various ways: body language, speech, the written (or increasingly now, the texted) word. However, whatever the medium chosen, the challenge is the same: to make clear, or occasionally to obscure, a message. The attempt is not always successful: in July 2007, the American journalist Ruth Marcus, reporting on the appearance of the then American Attorney-General, Alberto Gonzales, before a Senate Committee, wrote critically of 'his signature brand of inartful dodging – linguistic evasion, poorly executed'.

For many years, letter-writing was the preferred means of communication between friends. It was not without effort: 'I have made this letter longer only because I have not had time to make it shorter,' wrote the French philosopher and scientist Blaise Pascal in the seventeenth century. However, it could also be a pleasant occupation. In the nineteenth century, the British politician and writer Lord Morley described it as 'that most agreeable way of wasting time'.

Communication is a key concern of any interviewer. The veteran American journalist Edward R. Murrow once said, 'It has always seemed to me that the real art in this business is not so much moving information or guidance or policy ... The real art is to move it the last three feet in face-to-face conversation.' And a cartoon by the American cartoonist Peter Arno captures a moment in which communication is reduced to essentials. A man is shown flirting with a woman, and the caption reads, 'Tell me about yourself, your struggles, your dreams, your telephone number.' He may also have been following the advice of Scott Adams from the world of Dilbert: 'Smile, it confuses people.'

Unless one is a genius, it is best to aim at being intelligible.
– ANTHONY HOPE

Good communication is stimulating as black coffee, and just as hard to sleep after.
– ANNE MORROW LINDBERGH

All letters, methinks, should be as free and easy as one's discourse, not studied as an oration, nor made up of hard words like a charm.
– DOROTHY OSBORNE

The more we elaborate our means of communication, the less we communicate.
– J. B. PRIESTLEY

I used to tell my husband that, if he could make *me* understand something, it would be clear to all the other people in the country.
– ELEANOR ROOSEVELT

A diplomat is a person who can tell you to go to hell in such a way that you actually look forward to the trip.
– CASKIE STINNETT

* * *

Competition

see also Friendship, Sport, Success

Competition can bring out the best, as well as the worst, in rivals. In Sir Walter Scott's poem *The Lady of the Lake*, warriors are held to feel 'stern joy' when encountering 'foemen worthy of their steel'. A few decades before Scott, in 1788, his fellow-Scot Robert Burns wrote to a friend, 'To be overtopped in anything else, I can bear: but in the tests of generous love, I defy all mankind!' Eric Idle, asked to rate himself against other members of Monty Python, was quoted as saying, 'I guess you could say I was the sixth nicest.'

Theodore Roosevelt's approach to dealing with competition was practical: 'Don't hit at all if it is honourably possible to avoid hitting; but *never* hit soft.' He would probably have appreciated the dry assessment of Dean Rusk during the Cuban Missile Crisis: 'We're eyeball to eyeball, and I think the other fellow just blinked.'

'Man,' said the essayist Charles Lamb, 'is a gaming animal. He must always be trying to get the better in something or other.' A few decades later Arthur Hugh Clough, updating the Ten Commandments in his poem 'The Latest Decalogue', wrote, 'Thou shalt not covet, but tradition Approves all forms of competition.' However, some rivalries are provoked, or increased, by resentment. According to Erica Jong, 'Jealousy is all the fun you think they had.' And gamesmanship is an inevitable part of competition. Long before Stephen Potter invented that concept, the American golfer Walter Hagen was reputed to say genially to opponents, 'Who's going to be second?'

Generally speaking, one author is a mole to another. It is impossible for them to discover beauties in one another's works; they have eyes only for spots and blemishes.
– JOSEPH ADDISON

Rivalry adds so much to the charm of one's conquest.
– LOUISA MAY ALCOTT

I've number two on my car and I am the number two driver.
– LEWIS HAMILTON
(after he had finished second to his McLaren team mate Fernando Alonso in the Monaco Grand Prix)

I strove with none; for none was worth my strife.
– WALTER SAVAGE LANDOR

The healthiest competition occurs when average people win by putting in above-average efforts.
– COLIN POWELL

Nothing is ever done beautifully, which is done in rivalship.
– JOHN RUSKIN

Invincibility depends on one's self, the enemy's vulnerability on him.
– SUN TZU

* * *

Conversation

see also Communication

The American writer on etiquette, Emily Post, once set out her definition of the 'ideal conversation'. In her view it should be 'an exchange of thought, and not, as many of those who worry most about their shortcomings believe, an eloquent exhibition of wit or oratory'. She would probably not have approved the picture evoked by an exchange between Dr Johnson and his biographer James Boswell. Johnson had said with evident satisfaction 'Well, we had a good talk', to which Boswell responded, 'Yes, Sir, you tossed and gored several persons.' In the twentieth century, a character in Patrick O'Brian's *Master and Commander* series of novels gave the view that 'Question and answer is not a civilized form of conversation.'

Conversation with Dr Johnson must have been a daunting prospect. According to his old friend Mrs Thrale, 'Johnson's conversation was by much too strong for a person accustomed to obsequiousness and flattery; it was *mustard in a young child's mouth!*' But there are also other dangers. The classical writer Seneca warned, 'Conversation has a kind of charm about it, an insinuating and insidious something that elicits secrets from us just like love or liquor.' He would have recognized, across the centuries, Henry Fielding's summary that 'Love and scandal are the best sweeteners of tea.'

Many writers have enjoined care in choosing one's words. According to Confucius, 'For one word a man is often deemed to be wise, and for one word he is often deemed to be foolish. We should be careful indeed what we say.' The seventeenth-century French moralist Jean de la Bruyère warned, 'There are people who speak one moment before they think.' Jane Austen's Emma Woodhouse clearly had warnings of this kind in mind as she negotiated her way through a difficult exchange: 'Emma denied none of it in public, and agreed with none of it in private.'

True happiness ... arises, in the first place from the enjoyment of one's self; and in the next, from the friendship and conversation of a few select companions.
– JOSEPH ADDISON

My idea of good company is the company of clever, well-informed people who have a great deal of conversation.
– JANE AUSTEN

You shake someone's hand, you have a conversation, and somehow you're all bound together because you share your own common humanity in one short moment.
– RALPH FIENNES

The real in us is silent, the acquired is talkative.
– KAHLIL GIBRAN

Never get a mime talking. He won't stop.
– MARCEL MARCEAU

With thee conversing I forget all time.
– JOHN MILTON

She lacks the power of conversation but not the power of speech.
– GEORGE BERNARD SHAW

Each person's life is lived as a series of conversations.
– DEBORAH TANNEN

There is no such thing as conversation. It is an illusion. There are intersecting monologues, that is all.
– REBECCA WEST

* * *

Courage

see also **Determination**

'No coward soul is mine,' wrote Emily Brontë, and there are many quotations which extol the virtues, and the attractions, of courage. Robert Louis Stevenson referred to 'the bright face of danger' as something to be welcomed, and Ralph Waldo Emerson adjured his readers, 'Always do what you are afraid to do.' The narrator of Robert Browning's poem 'Prospice', telling us that he 'was ever a fighter', looked forward with enthusiasm to 'one fight more, The best and the last!'

For some, of course, this state of mind is less easily achieved. Lady Macbeth (admittedly for a reprehensible purpose) had to urge on her husband, 'But screw your courage to the sticking place.' Less seriously, Stephen Leacock reflected, 'It takes a good deal of physical courage to ride a horse. This, however, I have. I get it at about forty cents a flask, and take it as required.' And even when you have brought yourself to resolution, it may not last. In Sheridan's The Rivals, Bob Acres, contemplating the prospect of a duel, laments, 'My valour is certainly going! – it is sneaking off! – I feel it oozing out as it were at the palms of my hands!' He might have been comforted by Peter Ustinov's pragmatic comment, 'Courage is often lack of insight, whereas cowardice in many cases is based on good information.'

In the end, however, there seems to be a consensus that courage is not only desirable in itself, but is likely to be an essential ingredient for a tolerable life. As Harriet Beecher Stowe wrote in the nineteenth century, 'When you get into a tight place, and everything goes against you till it seems as if you couldn't hold on a minute longer, never give up then, for that's just the place and time that the tide'll turn.' A favourite piece of advice of the Confederate general Thomas 'Stonewall' Jackson was said to be, 'Never take counsel of your fears.'

Courage is the thing. All goes if courage goes.
– J. M. BARRIE

Risk comes from not knowing what you are doing.
– WARREN BUFFETT

Courage is the price that Life exacts for granting peace.
– AMELIA EARHART

Life is either a daring adventure, or nothing.
– HELEN KELLER

Do not lie, do not steal, and do not be afraid. Mainly, do not be afraid.
– JACK NICHOLSON
(advice for life)

Life shrinks or expands in proportion to one's courage.
– ANAÏS NIN

The future doesn't belong to the fainthearted, it belongs to the brave.
– RONALD REAGAN

The only thing we have to fear is fear itself.
– FRANKLIN ROOSEVELT

* * *

Criticism

see also Art, Music, Writing

Critics have not generally received a good press, although Matthew Arnold set out a strong position: 'I am bound by my own definition of criticism: a disinterested endeavour to learn and propagate the best that is known and thought in the world.' However, by the time that Arnold wrote this, in the middle of the nineteenth century, there was already a strong literary tradition of criticizing critics. Just over a hundred years earlier, Charles Churchill had written, 'Though by whim, envy, or resentment led, They damn those authors whom they never read.' Churchill's critics seem to have had an affinity with those evoked by Byron more than forty years later, who were well supplied with hackneyed jokes 'got by rote', and who had 'just enough of learning to misquote'.

To be a critic can be a thankless task. Dr Johnson thought that 'The man who is asked by an author what he thinks of his work, is put to the torture, and is not obliged to speak the truth.' Somerset Maugham pointed out that 'People ask you for criticism, but they only want praise.' The Finnish composer Sibelius suggested that no attention should be paid to what the critics say: 'No statue has ever been put up to a critic.'

The writer Christopher Hampton commented that 'Asking a working writer what he thinks about critics is like asking a lamp-post how it feels about dogs.' Kenneth Tynan, himself a noted theatre critic, recognized the limitations of his skills: 'A critic is a man who knows the way but can't drive the car.'

Criticism may not be agreeable, but it is necessary. It fulfils the same function as pain in the human body; it calls attention to the development of an unhealthy state of things.
– WINSTON CHURCHILL

Criticism, as it was first instituted by Aristotle, was meant a standard of judging well; the chiefest part of which is, to observe those excellencies, which should delight a reasonable reader.
– JOHN DRYDEN

A good critic is one who tells of his own soul's adventures among masterpieces.
– ANATOLE FRANCE

The pleasure of criticizing takes away from us the pleasure of being moved by some very fine things.
– JEAN DE LA BRUYÈRE

He has the right to criticize, who has the heart to help.
– ABRAHAM LINCOLN

The lot of critics is to be remembered by what they failed to understand.
– GEORGE MOORE

I never read a book before reviewing it; it prejudices a man so.
– SYDNEY SMITH

* * *

Curiosity

see also Education, Thought

'Curiosity', the proverb tells us, 'killed the cat', but indulging it may bring rewards as well as risks. In Kipling's *Just-So Stories*, the Elephant's Child who persistently asks questions acquires a trunk as a direct result of his "satiable curtiosity'. Curiosity, with an expectation of a pleasurable answer, surely lies behind Charles Lamb's comment that 'Not many sounds in life, and I include all urban and rural sounds, exceed in interest a knock at the door.'

Curiosity about what is not your business, of course, is likely to be discouraged. The child in Kipling's 'Smuggler's Song', told to 'watch the wall, my darling, while the Gentlemen go by' is warned, 'Don't you ask no questions, and you'll be told no lies.' Lewis Carroll's Duchess told Alice cross-ly that 'If everybody minded their own business, the world would go round a good deal faster than it does.' As Jonathan Swift once wrote, 'A person who is too nice an observer of the business of the crowd, like one who is too curious in observing the labour of the bees, will often be stung for his curiosity.'

But intellectual enquiry is a different thing. Dr Johnson thought that 'A generous and elevated mind is distinguished by nothing more certainly than an eminent degree of curi-osity.' Dylan Thomas, writing of Christmases in his Welsh boyhood, expressed his sense of frustration on receiving a book which told him 'everything about the wasp, except why'.

The one real object of education is to have a man in the condition of continually asking questions.
– MANDELL CREIGHTON

The wise man is not the man who gives the right answers; he is the one who asks the right questions.
– CLAUDE LÉVI-STRAUSS

Curiosity is the key to creativity.
– AKIO MORITA

Life was meant to be lived. Curiosity must be kept alive.
– ELEANOR ROOSEVELT

Curiosity will conquer fear even more than bravery will.
– JAMES STEPHENS

Disinterested intellectual curiosity is the life blood of real civilization.
– G. M. TREVELYAN

* * *

Cyberspace

see also Communication, Progress, Technology

In 1953, the American business executive Thomas J.Watson Jnr noted at IBM's annual stockholders' meeting that a sales trip for the newly-introduced (and very costly) Electronic Data Processing Machine had resulted in orders for eighteen machines, rather than the five they had expected. Over time, this has been transmuted into what appears to have been a startlingly wrong prediction: 'I think there is a world market for about five computers.'

Over fifty years later, it is already hard to imagine a world without computers, although Noam Chomsky has reminded us that 'The Internet is an elite organization; most of the population of the world has never even made a phone call.' The actress Judi Dench, questioned about her use of email, replied regretfully, 'I am afraid it is a non-starter. I cannot even use a bicycle pump.' The American academic Robert Wilensky has also commented sardonically on the benefits of online access: 'We've all heard that a million monkeys

73

banging on a million typewriters will eventually produce the works of Shakespeare. Now, thanks to the Internet, we know this is not true.' The online world has also contributed to our stock of modern sayings: older formulations such as 'Garbage in, garbage out' and 'What you see is what you get' have now been joined by the somewhat defensive 'That's not a bug, that's a feature.' And the co-founder of the World Wide Web, Robert Cailliau, has pointed out a particular deficiency of the cyberworld: 'There is no such thing as a virtual beer.'

A computer terminal is not some clunky old television with a typewriter in front of it. It is an interface where the mind and body can connect with the universe and move bits of it about.
– Douglas Adams

The Internet is becoming the town square for the village that the world will be tomorrow.
– Bill Gates

I think computer viruses should count as life. I think it says something about human nature that the only form of life we have created so far is purely destructive. We've created life in our own image.
– Stephen Hawking

Don't explain computers to laymen. Simpler to explain sex to a virgin.
– Robert Heinlein

74

Do you want to spend the rest of your life selling sugared water or do you want a chance to change the world?
– STEVE JOBS
(persuading John Sculley, then President of Pepsico, to move
 to Apple Computers)

Computing is not about computers any more. It is about living.
– NICHOLAS NEGROPONTE

*   *   *

Death

see also Bereavement, Grief, Love

'Golden lads and girls all must As chimney sweepers, come to dust', lines from the song in Shakespeare's *Cymbeline*, acknowledge the finality, and inevitability, of death. In the seventeenth century, Jean de la Fontaine noted, 'Death does not take the wise man by surprise, he is always prepared to leave.' A century before, Francis Bacon found death 'the least of all evils', although he also understood that 'Men fear death as children fear to go in the dark; and as that natural fear in children is increased with tales, so is the other.' Or, as Professor Dumbledore was to tell Harry Potter, 'It is the unknown we fear when we look upon death and darkness, nothing more.'

There are various comforts to be found against this fear of the unknown. 'My name is Death, the last best friend am

I,' wrote the poet Robert Southey, and the nineteenth-century writer and socialite the Countess of Blessington gave an account of how this could be: 'It is better to die young than to outlive all one loved, and all that rendered one lovable.' In the twentieth century, Stevie Smith spoke for the idea of a relief from the stresses of life: 'If there wasn't death, I think you couldn't go on.' When Ingmar Bergman died in 2007, his obituary in the New York Times quoted his comment, 'When I was young, I was extremely scared of dying. But now I think it a very, very wise arrangement. It's like a light that is extinguished. Not very much to make a fuss about.' And yet, against this echo of the biblical 'O death, where is thy sting? O grave, where is thy victory?' we also acknowledge the force of John Donne's assertion that 'No man is an island entire of itself ... any man's death diminishes me, because I am involved in mankind.'

Why fear death? It is the most beautiful adventure in life.
– CHARLES FROHMAN
(last words of the producer of Peter Pan before going down
 with the Lusitania)

Death is nothing at all. I have only slipped away into the next room. I am I and you are you. Whatever we were to each other, that we are still.
– HENRY SCOTT HOLLAND

People living deeply have no fear of death.
– ANAÏS NIN

For death is no more than a turning of us over from time to eternity.
– WILLIAM PENN

The last stages of life should not be seen as defeat, but rather as life's fulfilment.
– CICELY SAUNDERS

Death must be distinguished from dying, with which it is often confused.
– SYDNEY SMITH

* * *

Departure

see also Arrival, Retirement

The departure of someone we love can be seen as a matter of desolation. 'My life will be sour grapes and ashes without you,' declares one of the characters in the child author Daisy Ashford's *The Young Visiters*. In the eighteenth century, the poet William Cowper thought that 'Absence from whom we love is worse than death' – an assertion that refuses the comfort offered by the proverbial 'Absence makes the heart grow fonder.' Reluctance to part is reflected in Robert Burns's 'Ae fond kiss, and then we sever!' 'Parting is such sweet sorrow,' cried Juliet to Romeo, and a few centuries later the poet Emily Dickinson wrote that 'Parting is all we know of heaven, And all we need of hell.'

Not all departures, of course, are associated with love or romance. 'Go where glory waits you,' wrote the Irish poet Thomas Moore (while adding the reminder, 'Oh! still remember me'). In the First World War, men were seen off to the front to the chant of Paul Alfred Rubens's song, 'We don't want to lose you, but we think you ought to go.'

With both Moore and Rubens, we have the sense of the person addressed being sent away. Sometimes, however, a person may choose to move on. The actress Helen Hayes is said to have explained a career move in the following terms: 'I'm leaving the screen because I don't think I am very good in the pictures and I have this beautiful dream that I'm elegant on the stage.'

'Tis distance lends enchantment to the view.
– Thomas Campbell

'Tis a strange truth that only in the agony of parting we look into the depths of love.
– George Eliot

Leaving is dying a little.
– Edmond Haraucourt

Will ye no' come back again?
– Lady Nairne
(the refrain of a song expressing the hope that Bonnie
 Prince Charlie might return from exile)

Absence diminishes mediocre passions and increases great ones, as the wind extinguishes candles and kindles fire.
– LA ROCHEFOUCAULD

Every separation gives a foretaste of death, – and every reunion a foretaste of resurrection.
– ARTHUR SCHOPENHAUER

There is a time for departure even when there's no certain place to go.
– TENNESSEE WILLIAMS

* * *

Determination

see also Courage, Success

'The die is cast,' said Julius Caesar, as he prepared to cross the Rubicon with his army, and other voices evoke the sense of an irrevocable decision. The nineteenth-century American admiral David Farragut is said to have given the order, 'Damn the torpedoes! Go ahead!'

Determination of course is not always well founded. As the eighteenth-century writer Laurence Sterne said, ''Tis known by the name of perseverance in a good cause, – and of obstinacy in a bad one.' Nevertheless, Winston Churchill made a strong case for not being readily deterred: 'Never submit to failure. Do not be fobbed off with mere personal success or acceptance. You will make all kinds of mistakes; but as long as you are generous and true, and also fierce, you cannot hurt the world.' Apparent failure can in fact have a positive side, as asserted in a quotation attributed to Thomas Edison: 'When I have eliminated the ways that will not work, I will find the way that will work.' The feminist Susan B. Anthony, addressing a meeting of the National Woman Suffrage Association at a celebration of her eighty-sixth birthday in 1906, said simply, 'Failure is impossible.'

No adversity is insurmountable. Regardless of the odds, I know that with hard work and dedication I can achieve anything.
– AMY ALSOP
(speaking for the Canadian team at the 2004 Paralympic Games)

Never give in, never never never ... except to convictions of honour and good sense.
– WINSTON CHURCHILL

The best way out is always through.
– ROBERT FROST

We will find a way, or make one.
– HANNIBAL
(crossing the Alps with his army)

No one ever drowned in his own sweat.
– ANN LANDERS

When you get to the end of your rope, tie a knot and hang on.
– FRANKLIN ROOSEVELT

* * *

Diets

see also Food

Warnings against overeating go back to the classical world. According to Pliny, 'Simple diet is the best; heaping up of several meats is pernicious, and sauces worse; many dishes bring many diseases.' This particular passage was quoted by the seventeenth-century writer Robert Burton in his *The Anatomy of Melancholy*. Burton, having commented approvingly on Pliny's approach, went on to list the (many) foods which he thought it best to avoid. These included 'all cakes, simnels, buns' as well as 'cracknels made with butter' and 'fritters, pancakes, pies, sausages, and ... sauces'.

In the eighteenth century, Benjamin Franklin offered the simple advice, 'To lengthen thy life, lessen thy meals.' He would have accepted the phenomenon noted by Walter de la Mare that 'Whatever Miss T eats Turns into Miss T.' However, it is clear that many people have difficulty in adopting what they may regard as a Spartan regime. Bertrand Russell

81

told the story of 'a noble lord who had had serious losses'. He asked a friend to recommend ways in which he could cut costs, and in due course received the advice that to keep three pastry-cooks was excessive. Russell records the peer's plaintive response: 'But hang it all, my dear fellow, a man must have a biscuit.' And it seems likely that no attempts at all were made by the character of whom P. G. Wodehouse wrote, 'The Right Hon was a tubby little chap who looked as if he had been poured into his clothes and had forgotten to say "When!".' Perhaps he shared the robust approach exemplified by a comment attributed to Mae West: 'I never worry about diets. The only carrots that interest me are the number you get in a diamond.'

If I can't have too many truffles, I'll do without truffles.
– COLETTE

Never eat more than you can lift.
– JIM HENSON
(Miss Piggy's advice)

I feel about airplanes the way I feel about diets. It seems to me that they are wonderful things for other people to go on.
– JEAN KERR

People don't have to be greedy, but it seems to me that life is a whole lot better if you enjoy food.
– NIGELLA LAWSON

Food is an important part of a balanced diet.
– FRAN LEBOWITZ

The biggest seller is cookbooks and the second is diet books – how not to eat what you've just learned to cook.
– ANDY ROONEY

* * *

Dogs

see also Cats

Comments about 'man's best friend' are not necessarily enthusiastic. The French revolutionary Madame Roland said, 'The more I see of men, the more I like dogs.' However, Aldous Huxley had an explanation for why people like dogs: 'To his dog, every man is Napoleon; hence the constant popularity of dogs.' Although John Sparrow might have taken issue with the idea of the 'constant popularity' of the dog: he described it as 'that indefatigable and unsavoury engine of pollution'.

Not all people who approach dogs courteously are declared dog-lovers. In George Eliot's novel *Middlemarch*, we hear of Dorothea that 'She was always attentive to the feelings of dogs, and very polite if she had to decline their advances.' A saying from modern American politics suggests a qualified enthusiasm: 'If you want a friend in Washington, buy a dog.'

Dogs may also be seen as likely to be a disruptive influence to a peaceful life. Lord Macaulay (having witnessed a dogfight) thought it 'odd that people of sense should find any pleasure in being accompanied by a beast who is always spoiling conversation'. Ogden Nash suggested that 'A door is what a dog is perpetually on the wrong side of.' And dog-owners come in for criticism too: the dramatist August Strindberg said, 'I loathe people who keep dogs. They are cowards who haven't got the guts to bite people themselves.'

A dog teaches a boy fidelity, perseverance, and to turn around three times before lying down.
– ROBERT BENCHLEY

The greatest pleasure of a dog is that you may make a fool of yourself with him, and not only will he not scold you, but he will make a fool of himself, too.
– SAMUEL BUTLER

Beauty without vanity, strength without insolence, courage without ferocity, and all the virtues of man without his vices.
– LORD BYRON
(epitaph on his Newfoundland dog)

Dogs will come when called ... Cats take a message and get back to you.
– MISSY DIZICK AND MARY BLY

The dog is a Yes-animal, very popular with people who can't afford to keep a Yes-man.
– ROBERTSON DAVIES

No one appreciates the very special genius of your conversation as a dog does.
– CHRISTOPHER MORLEY

My little old dog: A heart-beat At my feet.
– EDITH WHARTON

* * *

Drink

see also Food

In the 1920s, Wodehouse's Bertie Wooster recalled that 'It was my Uncle George who discovered that alcohol was a food in advance of modern medical thought.' The implication seems to be that Uncle George was not particularly concerned about the form in which his chosen food arrived, but others have been more discriminating. Dr Johnson, indeed, allocated particular drinks to particular qualities: 'Claret is the liquor for boys; port for men; but he who aspires to be a hero must drink brandy.' Robert Burns suggested that 'Freedom and whisky gang thegither.' A. E. Housman's Shropshire Lad, eschewing wine and spirits, turned to beer: 'And malt does more than Milton can To justify God's words to man.' It was not an approach that would have appealed to the character in George Bernard Shaw's play *Candida*, who warned, 'I'm only a beer teetotaller, not a champagne teetotaller.'

The great Canadian physician William Osler is quoted as describing alcohol as 'milk of the elderly', but the dangers of drink have also been stressed. In the seventeenth century, Robert Burton wrote, 'I may not omit those two main plagues, and common dotages of human kind, wine and women, which have infatuated and besotted myriads of people. They go commonly together.' However, against this rather puritanical approach there are a number of personal statements in support of alcohol. Thomas Love Peacock, in the nineteenth century, wrote, 'There are two reasons for drinking; one is, when you are thirsty, to cure it; the other, when you are not thirsty, to prevent it ... Prevention is better than cure.' Or, as the character in Rabelais' *Gargantua* said in the sixteenth century, 'I drink for the thirst to come.'

I only take a drink on two occasions: when I'm thirsty and when I'm not.
– BRENDAN BEHAN

Alcohol is like love: the first kiss is magic, the second is intimate, the third is routine. After that you just take the girl's clothes off.
– RAYMOND CHANDLER

A well-balanced person has a drink in each hand.
– BILLY CONNOLLY

Champagne, if you are seeking the truth, is better than a lie-detector. It encourages a man to be expansive, even reckless, while lie-detectors are only a challenge to tell lies successfully.
– GRAHAM GREENE

Come quickly, I am tasting stars!
– DOM PERIGNON
(allegedly, on inventing champagne)

Wine is bottled poetry.
– ROBERT LOUIS STEVENSON

When I read about the evils of drinking, I gave up reading.
– HENNY YOUNGMAN

* * *

Education

see also Examinations, Teaching

In the film *Iris*, the frail Iris Murdoch, watching a television report of the Labour Party Conference which featured the keynote speech by Tony Blair, asked worriedly, 'Why is he repeating himself?' The year was 1996, and the then Leader of the Opposition was telling his party, 'Ask me my three main priorities for Government, and I tell you: education, education and education.'

The repetition was of course a rhetorical device for emphasis rather than a symptom of mental confusion, and it was foreshadowed in the writing of the nineteenth-century French historian Jules Michelet, 'What is the first part of politics? Education. The second? Education. And the third? Education.'

While education itself is seen to be a positive, there are different ways in which it can be delivered. One of the less attractive is found in Dickens's account of Mr Wackford Squeers's establishment, Dotheboys Hall. As Mr Squeers explained the system to Nicholas Nickleby: 'C-l-e-a-n, clean, verb active, to make bright, to scour. W-i-n, win, d-e-r, der, winder, a casement. When the boy knows this out of the book, he goes and does it.' It seems unlikely that the recipient of this kind of education would have agreed with the view of the philosopher Herbert Spencer that 'Education has for its object the formation of character.'

One way of avoiding the terrors of Dotheboys Hall might have been to follow the path of self-education – something endorsed by the writer Sir Walter Scott: 'All men who have turned out worth anything have had the chief hand in their own education.'

I read Shakespeare and the Bible and I can shoot dice. That's what I call a liberal education.
– TALLULAH BANKHEAD

To live for a time close to great minds is the best kind of education.
– JOHN BUCHAN

I've over-educated myself in all the things I shouldn't
have known at all.
– NOËL COWARD

Education is not preparation for life, education is life
itself.
– JOHN DEWEY

Thank goodness, my education was neglected; I was
never sent to school ... It would have rubbed off some of
the originality.
– BEATRIX POTTER

Get informed. Get outraged. Get inspired. Get active.
– ANITA RODDICK

*   *   *

Examinations

see also Education

'Examinations,' said the English clergyman and essayist
Charles Caleb Colton, 'are formidable even to the best prepared, for the greatest fool may ask more than even the wis-
est man may answer.' Without necessarily including themselves in the category of the most wise, many candidates have
found an examination paper formidable, or at least daunting. Winston Churchill has left us an account of taking the

entrance examination for Harrow: 'I wrote my name at the top of the page. I wrote down the number of the question "1". After much reflection I put a bracket round it thus "(1)". But thereafter I could not think of anything connected with it that was either relevant or true.' He thought it very creditable to the headmaster that he was admitted to Harrow on 'these slender indications of scholarship'. His success contrasts with that of the miner in *Beyond the Fringe*. As played by Peter Cook, he lamented, 'I could have been a judge, but I never had the Latin. I just never had sufficient of it to get through the rigorous judging exams.'

Some responsibility, of course, rests with those who set examination papers. The critic and academic George Saintsbury quoted unadmiringly from a literature paper, 'Without remarking that the thing became a trumpet in his hands, say something relevant about Milton's sonnets.' It is possible to imagine a baffled candidate feeling the need of the helpful advice given in Sellar and Yeatman's *1066 and All That*: 'Do not on any account attempt to write on both sides of the paper at once.'

I was thrown out ... for cheating on my metaphysics final ... I looked within the soul of the boy sitting next to me.
– WOODY ALLEN AND MARSHALL BRICKMAN
(from *Annie Hall*, 1977, spoken by Woody Allen)

I know that if I'd had to go and take an exam for acting, I wouldn't have got anywhere. You don't take exams for acting, you take your courage.
– EDITH EVANS

You treat scripts as an exam-paper and yourself, somewhat arrogantly, as the examiner. For films, the pass-mark is 55 per cent.
– JOHN HURT

Exams work because they're scary.
– BORIS JOHNSON

I had never passed a single school exam, and clearly never would.
– MARY LEAKEY

In examinations the foolish ask questions that the wise cannot answer.
– OSCAR WILDE

* * *

Families

see also Babies, Children

'Treasure your families' advised Pope John Paul II, adding that 'the future of humanity passes by way of the family'. Other commentators, however, have been more likely to focus on difficulties prevalent in family life. In the sixteenth century, Montaigne commented that 'There is scarcely any less trouble in running a family than in governing an entire state.' (Domestic matters, while being less important, were 'no less importunate'.) The seventeenth-century clergyman Jeremy Taylor gave a warning of what might develop from an unhappy family: 'He that loves not his wife and children, feeds a lioness at home and broods a nest of sorrows.' As President of the United States, George H. W. Bush reached for fictional families to express his concerns for American society: 'We're going to strengthen the American family: to make them more like the Waltons and less like the Simpsons.'

Family life has its own strains. The nineteenth-century novelist R. S. Surtees evoked a moment of sibling rivalry: 'The young ladies entered the drawing-room in the full fervour of sisterly animosity.' In the twentieth century, the American writer Shirley Jackson put forward the view that 'in times of great stress, such as a four-day vacation, the thin veneer of family wears off almost at once, and we are revealed in our true personalities'.

Family pride has its place, but not everyone can live up to it. In the Marx Brothers film *Horse Feathers*, a character is reproached, 'You're a disgrace to our family name of Wagstaff, if such a thing is possible.' And the representative of a very distinguished family indeed, Queen Elizabeth II, has said ruefully, 'Like all the best families, we have our share of eccentricities, of impetuous and wayward youngsters and of family disagreements.'

The presidency is temporary – but the family is permanent.
– YVONNE DE GAULLE

The only rock I know that stays steady, the only institution I know that works, is the family.
– LEE IACOCCA

I was born Beatrice Gladys Lillie at an extremely tender age because my mother needed a fourth at meals.
– BEATRICE LILLIE

No matter how many communes anybody invents, the family always creeps back.
– MARGARET MEAD

The great advantage of living in a large family is that early lesson of life's essential unfairness.
– NANCY MITFORD

I find myself surprised at how its realism actually unites morality with – yes – romance. It is that need that draws us to nest in rows, separated by thin walls, hoping to be tolerated and loved forever – and to go on reproducing ourselves in family patterns, handing on some misery (perhaps), but untold happiness too.
– BEL MOONEY

If you cannot get rid of the family skeleton, you may as well make it dance.
– GEORGE BERNARD SHAW

All happy families resemble one another, but every unhappy family is unhappy in its own way.
– LEO TOLSTOY

It is no use telling me that there are bad aunts and good aunts. At the core they are all alike. Sooner or later out pops the cloven hoof.
– P. G. WODEHOUSE

* * *

Fashion

see also Appearance

'One had as good be out of the world, as out of fashion,' was the view of a character in Colley Cibber's play *Love's Last Shift*, and this dictum from the late seventeenth century may well find echoes today. The approval is not, though, universal: the view of the Australian poet and writer Les Murray was that 'In the defiance of fashion is the beginning of character.'

Even those who spend their lives in the world of fashion may have reservations. The photographer David Bailey confessed, 'I never cared for fashion much, amusing little seams and witty little pleats: it was the girls I liked.' Cecil Beaton, horrified at the advent of the miniskirt, said that 'Never in the history of fashion has so little material been raised so high to reveal so much that needs to be covered so badly.' He might have found an explanation in a comment by Coco

Chanel: 'Fashion is reduced to a question of hem lengths. Haute couture is finished because it's in the hands of men who don't like women.'

For the ordinary person wishing (with Colley Cibber's character) to be in fashion, there have been various pieces of advice. Beau Brummel, who set the tone for the early nineteenth century, had a very practical approach: 'No perfumes, but very fine linen, plenty of it, and country washing.' It may matter who you are. In the 1920s world of Anita Loos' gold-digging siren Lorelei Lee, we find the judgement, 'You have got to be a Queen to get away with a hat like that.'

Fashion anticipates, and elegance is a state of mind.
– OLEG CASSINI

Fashion is made to become unfashionable.
– COCO CHANEL

I dress for the image. Not for myself, not for the public, not for fashion, not for men.
– MARLENE DIETRICH

I don't design clothes. I design dreams.
– RALPH LAUREN

I base most of my fashion taste on what doesn't itch.
– GILDA RADNER

Fashion passes; style is eternal.
– YVES SAINT LAURENT

You can say what you like about long dresses, but they cover a multitude of shins.
– MAE WEST

Hats divide generally into three classes: offensive hats, defensive hats, and shrapnel.
– KATHARINE WHITEHORN

* * *

Fathers

see also Children, Families, Mothers, Parents

While a good deal has been written and said in praise of motherhood, views of fatherhood are often more temperate. Lord Chesterfield, writing in the eighteenth century, was objective rather than enthusiastic: 'As fathers commonly go, it is seldom a misfortune to be fatherless; and considering the general run of sons, as seldom a misfortune to be child-less.' On the other hand, the Victorian narrative picture 'And when did you last see your father?', showing the small son of a Royalist family facing Parliamentary officers, implies love and loyalty felt by the child for the absent parent.

Wars, civil or otherwise, have often separated fathers and their children. The broadcaster John Peel, born in 1939, described the effect for a small child of having a father who was away from home on active service: 'Father, I decided, probably didn't exist at all, remaining, for the first six years of my life, a figure as remote and improbable as the characters in the *Blue Fairy Book*.'

Fathers who were present could be alarming. In Thomas Campbell's ballad, Lord Ullin's daughter, eloping with her lover and pursued by her father, makes the disastrous decision to cross a swollen river in an inadequate boat: 'I'll meet the raging of the skies, But not an angry father.' Lord Ullin, arriving too late, could only watch and lament as his daughter drowned. A very different approach to fatherhood was shown by Theodore Roosevelt, also father to a lively and determined daughter. As President of the United States, he is said to have commented resignedly, 'I can run the country or manage Alice but not both.'

Fatherhood is pretending that the present you love most is soap-on-a-rope.
– BILL COSBY

The fundamental defect of fathers is that they want their children to be a credit to them.
– BERTRAND RUSSELL

It doesn't matter who my father was; it matters who I remember he was.
– ANNE SEXTON

All the feeling which my father could not put into words was in his hand – any dog, child or horse would recognize the kindness of it.
– FREYA STARK

No man is responsible for his father. That is entirely his mother's affair.
– MARGARET TURNBULL

When I was a boy of fourteen my father was so ignorant I could hardly stand to have the old man around. But when I got to be twenty-one, I was astonished at how much he had learned in seven years.
– MARK TWAIN

* * *

Film

see also Acting

'The movies', said the American humorist Will Rogers, 'are the only business where you can go out front and applaud yourself.' Other commentators have considered the difficulties of the world of the silver screen. The screenwriter William Goldman opened his memoir of Hollywood, *Adventures in the Screen Trade*, with the words 'Nobody knows anything.' The American pianist Oscar Levant predicted, 'Strip the phoney tinsel off Hollywood and you'll find the real tinsel underneath.' The feared gossip columnist and former actress Hedda Hopper wrote that 'In Hollywood gratitude is Public Enemy Number One.' And as Sam Goldwyn is supposed to have said, it was a world in which 'Directors are always biting the hand that lays the golden egg.'

Cary Grant is quoted as taking a very unglamorous look at the film world. 'We have our factory, which is called a stage. We make a product, we colour it, we title it and we ship it out in cans.' Woody Allen, on the other hand, has said, 'My films are therapy for my debilitating depression. In institutions, people weave baskets. I make films.' Less prosaic descriptions include the theatre critic Kenneth Tynan's assertion that 'The cinema has no boundaries. It's a ribbon of dream', and Jean Cocteau's 'A film is a petrified fountain of thought.'

In 1991, an obituary for Frank Capra quoted him as saying that 'There are no rules in film-making. Only sins; and the cardinal sin is dullness.' Alfred Hitchcock warned of another danger: 'The length of a film should be directly related to the endurance of the human bladder.'

Film-making is a chance to live many lifetimes.
– ROBERT ALTMAN

All I need to make a comedy is a park, a policeman and a pretty girl.
– CHARLIE CHAPLIN

The trouble with this business is the dearth of bad pictures.
– SAM GOLDWYN

**There are only three ages for women in Hollywood
– Babe, District Attorney and Driving Miss Daisy.**
– GOLDIE HAWN

**If I made Cinderella people would be looking for the
body in the coach.**
– ALFRED HITCHCOCK

I dream for a living.
– STEVEN SPIELBERG

* * *

Fishing

see also Leisure, Sport

One of the most famous sources of comments on fishing comes from the seventeenth century: Izaak Walton's *The Compleat Angler* (1653). In writing of his chosen pastime, Walton reached back for comparison to a saying of William Butler, royal physician of the early seventeenth century. He wrote, 'We may say of angling as Dr Boteler said of straw-berries: "Doubtless God could have made a better berry, but doubtless God never did"; and so (if I might be judge) God never did make a more calm, quiet, innocent recreation than angling.' He backed up his view with further quotation, this time from the diplomat Henry Wotton, who asserted that 'it was an employment for his idle time, which was then not idly spent'. Wotton characterized fishing as 'a diverter of sadness, a calmer of unquiet thoughts, a moderator of passions, a procurer of contentedness'.

Not everyone, of course, would find the same pleasure in fishing. Dr Johnson's approval of it was strictly, and specifically, limited: 'Fly fishing may be a very pleasant amusement; but angling or float fishing I can only compare to a stick and a string, with a worm at one end and a fool at the other.' And in the eighteenth century, John Wolcot, writing under the pseudonym of 'Peter Pindar', spoke up on behalf of the fish. Envisioning the situation in which an angler, 'through gluttony's vile sin', attempted to pull the 'harmless fish' from its stream, he concluded, 'God give thee strength, O gentle trout, To pull the rascal in!' It is a situation which finds an echo in a rueful comment made by Queen Elizabeth the Queen Mother, herself a notable angler. Hospitalized after a fishbone lodged in her throat, she remarked wryly, 'The salmon are striking back.'

I love fishing. You put that line in the water and you don't know what's on the other end. Your imagination's under there.
– ROBERT ALTMAN

If fishing is a religion, fly fishing is high church.
– TOM BROKAW

I love fishing. It's like transcendental meditation with a punch-line.
– BILLY CONNOLLY

There is only one theory about angling in which I have perfect confidence, and this is that the two words, least appropriate to any statement about it, are the words 'always' and 'never'.
– LORD GREY

In our family, there was no clear line between religion and fly fishing.
– NORMAN MACLEAN

It has always been my private conviction that any man who pits his intelligence against a fish and loses has it coming.
– JOHN STEINBECK

* * *

Food

see also Diets, Drink, Hospitality

'The discovery of a new dish does more for the happiness of mankind than the discovery of a star,' said the French gastronome Anthelme Brillat-Savarin, although the discovery itself may require courage. As Thomas Fuller wrote in the seventeenth century, 'He was a very valiant man who first ventured on eating oysters.' Many commentators have dwelt affectionately on a particular kind of food. The process of cookery is not necessarily involved. Elizabeth David wrote that 'To eat figs off the tree in the very early morning, when they have been barely touched by the sun, is one of the exquisite pleasures of the Mediterranean.' Less romantically, but with equal warmth, the marooned Ben Gunn in Robert Louis Stevenson's *Treasure Island* recalled, 'Many's the long night I have dreamed of cheese – toasted mostly.'

Ben Gunn had at least a limited form of cookery in mind, although not of the kind that would have met the standards set by the nineteenth-century cook Eliza Acton: 'The difference between good and bad cookery can scarcely be more strikingly shown than in the manner in which sauces are prepared and served.' She would have sympathized with Delia Smith's comment on cooking with a microwave, 'I think it takes the soul out of food. Cooking is about ingredients being put together, and having time to amalgamate.' Acton's contemporary Thomas Hood, on the other hand, probably had in mind someone who would not have passed her test when he wrote of 'Home-made dishes that drive one from home'.

It is not only home cooking that can come in for criticism. The architect Sir Edwin Lutyens was in a restaurant when he made the resigned comment, 'This piece of cod passes all understanding.' And a particular kind of food may be seen as beyond redemption – as cucumber evidently was for Dr Johnson: 'A cucumber should be well sliced, and dressed with pepper and vinegar, and then thrown out, as good for nothing.'

Tell me what you eat and I will tell you what you are.
– ANTHELME BRILLAT-SAVARIN

Cookery without meat is Macbeth without murder.
– A. A. GILL

Cuisine is when things taste like what they are.
– PRUE LEITH

All I am I owe to spaghetti.
– SOPHIA LOREN

Many kids can tell you about drugs but do not know what celery or courgettes taste like.
– JAMIE OLIVER

The noblest of all dogs is the hot-dog. It feeds the hand that bites it.
– LAURENCE J. PETER

A good cook is like a sorceress who dispenses happiness.
– ELSA SCHIAPARELLI

* * *

Friendship

see also Relationships

'Of all the means to ensure happiness through out the whole of life, by far the most important is the acquisition of friends,' said the Greek philosopher Epicurus. Many centuries later,

Francis Bacon put it simply: 'It is the worst solitude, to have no true friendships.' Byron thought that 'Friendship is Love without his wings.'

In the seventeenth century, the French soldier and writer the Comte de Bussy-Rabutin wrote that 'Love springs from blindness, friendship from knowledge.' Such knowledge, however, can present difficulties. The eighteenth-century politician George Canning put it neatly in a couplet: 'But of all plagues, good Heaven, thy wrath can send, Save me, oh, save me, from the candid friend.' George Eliot indicated the possible impact of such candour when she wrote, 'Animals are such agreeable friends – they ask no questions, they pass no criticism.' The American Union general, William Tecumseh Sherman, once explained his friendship and support for his fellow general Ulysses S. Grant as being based on mutual knowledge and understanding: 'He stood by me when I was crazy and I stood by him when he was drunk. And now, sir, we stand by each other always.'

There are some distinctive views as to the test of friendship. Samuel Johnson commented, 'How few of his friends' houses would a man choose to be at when he is sick.' In the twentieth century, Logan Pearsall Smith said, 'I might give my life for my friend, but he had better not ask me to do up a parcel.' The French novelist Colette noted, 'My true friends have always given me that supreme proof of devotion, a spontaneous aversion for the man I loved.' Bing Crosby is on record with a neatly double-edged accolade on his relationship with Bob Hope: 'There is nothing in the world I wouldn't do for Hope, and there is nothing he wouldn't do for me ... We spend our lives doing nothing for each other.'

In the end, however, friendship is seen as one of the essentials of life. As W. B. Yeats wrote, 'Say my glory was I had such friends.'

No man is a failure who has friends.
(a line from the film *It's a Wonderful Life* (1946))

There is no desert like living without friends. Friendship multiplies the good of life, and divides the evil.
– BALTASAR GRACIAN

If a man does not make new acquaintance as he advances through life, he will soon find himself left alone. A man, Sir, should keep his friendship in constant repair.
– SAMUEL JOHNSON

Friendship is unnecessary, like philosophy, like art ... It has no survival value; rather it is one of those things that give value to survival.
– C. S. LEWIS

True friendship is a plant of slow growth, and must undergo and withstand the shocks of adversity before it is entitled to the appellation.
– GEORGE WASHINGTON

I no doubt deserved my enemies, but I don't believe I deserved my friends.
– WALT WHITMAN

* * *

The Future

see also Past, Present, Time

Ambrose Bierce, in a characteristically cynical definition, called the future 'that period of time in which our affairs prosper, our friends are true and our happiness is assured'. Albert Camus wrote grimly that 'The future is the only kind of property that the masters willingly concede to slaves.' This association of the future with the unreal, and its dangers, was evoked by Quentin Crisp in his autobiography: 'I still lived in the future – a habit which is the death of happiness.' Or, to quote from the song by the American radical Joe Hill, 'You'll get pie in the sky when you die.'

Others have seen the future as threatening rather than inviting. George Orwell conjured up a horrific image: 'If you want a picture of the future, imagine a boot stamping on a human face – for ever.' Kenneth Clark, completing his television series *Civilization*, while not evoking such brutality, was unenthusiastic: 'One may be optimistic, but one can't exactly be joyful at the prospect before us.' The prospect is unavoidable: as C. S. Lewis's demon warned his nephew in *The Screwtape Letters*, 'The Future is something which everyone reaches at the rate of sixty minutes an hour, whatever he does, whoever he is.'

The effect of these comments is to suggest that the future is something that happens to us, and that we have little or no power over it. It has been dictated by what has already happened. As Marcel Proust wrote, 'What we call our future is the shadow which our past throws in front of us.' Another approach, however, is suggested by the scientist Alan Kay: 'The best way of predicting the future is to invent it.' And we can always take the positive approach, asserting with Scarlet O'Hara in the closing scene of *Gone With The Wind*, 'After all, tomorrow is another day.'

Study the past, if you would divine the future.
– CONFUCIUS

I have learned to live each day as it comes, and not to borrow trouble by dreading tomorrow. It is the dark menace of the future that makes cowards of us all.
– DOROTHY DIX

I never think of the future. It comes soon enough.
– ALBERT EINSTEIN

The future is already here – it's just unevenly distributed.
– WILLIAM GIBSON

Life wouldn't be worth living if I worried over the future as well as the present.
– W. Somerset Maugham

The future is made of the same stuff as the present.
– Simone Weil

The future is called 'perhaps', which is the only possible thing to call the future. And the important thing is not to allow that to scare you.
– Tennessee Williams

* * *

Gardens

see also **Home**

Gardening has a long pedigree. We are told in the Bible that 'The Lord God planted a garden, eastward in Eden.' In the seventeenth century, Abraham Cowley drew a contrast between this and less innocent foundations: 'God the first garden made, and the first city Cain.' A garden may be seen as offering something essential: Cicero evoked a situation in which food would be provided for body and mind by writing to a friend, 'If you have a garden in your library, we shall lack for nothing.' Edward Gibbon evidently found the proximity of a garden helpful to creativity: 'I wrote the last lines of the last page, in a summer-house in my garden.'

Enjoyment of a garden may involve a degree of sacrifice, or at least a certain amount of accommodation to the needs of others. The essayist Joseph Addison wrote in the eighteenth century, 'I value my garden more for being full of blackbirds than of cherries, and very frankly give them fruit for their songs.'

In our own time, Margaret Atwood has asserted that 'Gardening is not a rational act', but others have seen reason in planting. As one character of Sir Walter Scott's told another, 'Jock, when ye hae naething else to do, ye may be aye sticking in a tree; it will be growing, Jock, when ye're sleeping.' And setting posterity aside, the very act of gardening is recommended for the beneficial and therapeutic effects it can bring to the individual. As Ralph Waldo Emerson wrote, 'All my hurts, my garden spade can heal.'

No occupation is so delightful to me as the culture of the earth, and no culture comparable to that of the garden.
– THOMAS JEFFERSON

The love of gardening is a seed that once sown never dies.
– GERTRUDE JEKYLL

To dig one's own spade into one's own earth! Has life anything better to offer than this?
– BEVERLEY NICHOLS

The most noteworthy thing about gardeners is that they are always optimistic, always enterprising, and never satisfied ... They always look forward to doing better than they have ever done before.
– VITA SACKVILLE-WEST

We may think we are tending our garden, but of course, in many different ways, it is the garden and the plants that are nurturing us.
– JENNY UGLOW

Laying out grounds, as it is called, may be considered as a liberal art.
– WILLIAM WORDSWORTH

* * *

Generosity

'Don't trust first impulses; they are always generous,' said Talleyrand, with characteristic cynicism. He was presumably thinking of the risks of sacrificing self-interest, but another cautionary view is put in a comment frequently ascribed to the American critic and writer Claire Booth Luce: 'No good deed goes unpunished.'

The moral of Aesop's fable of 'The Lion and the Mouse' was that 'No act of kindness, no matter how small, is ever wasted.' In the eighteenth century, the politician Edmund Burke, thought that we should 'cultivate ... every sort of generous and honest feeling'. Burke also recommended an 'enlightened self-interest', perhaps something linked to the 'middle-class morality' deplored by George Bernard Shaw's Mr Doolittle as 'Just an excuse for never giving me anything.'

Against these warnings, or at best qualified approval, there can be set a long tradition of seeing generosity in a positive light unaffected by concern for oneself. A saying attributed to the Indian Emperor Asoka in the 3rd century BC runs: 'All men are my children. What I desire for my children ... I desire for all men.' Publilius Syrus, a Roman writer of the 1st century BC, has left us a saying that has become proverbial: 'He does the poor man two favours who gives quickly.'

We are told in the Bible that 'God loveth a cheerful giver', but some sensitivity may be required. And philanthrophy which is too public may also occasion comment. As Billy Connolly has commented of Andrew Carnegie: 'It was said that he gave away money as silently as a waiter falling down a flight of stairs with a tray of glasses.'

Never ascribe to an opponent motives meaner than your own.
– J. M. BARRIE

The manner of giving is worth more than the gift.
– PIERRE CORNEILLE

It is better to give than to lend, and it costs about the same.
– PHILIP GIBBS

As you grow older, you will discover that you have two hands: one for helping yourself, the other for helping others.
– AUDREY HEPBURN

Liberality consists less in giving a great deal than in gifts well timed.
– JEAN DE LA BRUYÈRE

The habit of giving only enhances the desire to give.
– WALT WHITMAN

* * *

God

see also Belief

The Bible tells us that 'with God all things are possible', but this is only one view of the Almighty. There may be limits even to omnipotence. 'Even God,' said the Athenian poet Agathon, 'is deprived of this one thing only: the power to undo what has been done.' The Victorian hymn writer A. C. Ainger's 'God is working his purpose out' offers an image of planned creation very different from Woody Allen's comment that God, while not evil, was 'basically an underachiever'.

Belief in God may be seen as essential. Rudyard Kipling in *Stalky & Co.* employed an anecdote about Benjamin Jowett, Master of Balliol. In the story, the much-tried Mr King recounts 'the shocking story of one Jowett ... who had told an atheistical undergraduate that if he could not believe in a Personal God by five that afternoon he would be expelled'. He was less tolerant than J. B. Priestley, who reflected on mid-twentieth-century discussions on religion that 'God can stand being told by Professor Ayer and Marghanita Laski that He doesn't exist.'

James Baldwin would have wanted reassurance as to the point of such belief: 'If the concept of God has any validity or any use, it can only be to make us larger, freer, and more loving. If God cannot do this, then it is time we got rid of him.' Others, however, simply take pleasure in the concept of the creator. As Picasso saw it, 'God is really only another artist. He invented the giraffe, the elephant, and the cat. He has no real style. He just goes on trying other things.'

If only God would give me some clear sign! Like making a large deposit in my name at a Swiss bank.
– WOODY ALLEN

A God who allowed us to prove his existence would be an idol.
– DIETRICH BONHOEFFER

God is like a skilful geometrician.
– THOMAS BROWNE

What God does, He does well.
– JEAN DE LA FONTAINE

Chance might be God's pseudonym when He does not want to sign his name.
– ANATOLE FRANCE

* * *

Grief

see also Bereavement, Death, Happiness

'Grief is the price we pay for love,' runs the modern saying, famously used in Queen Elizabeth's message read at the service held in Washington Cathedral to commemorate the victims of the September 11th 2001 terrorist attacks. Yet while grief is recognized as an inevitable part of the human condition, the ways in which it is expressed or experienced may vary widely from person to person.

In George Eliot's *Middlemarch*, Dorothea recognized a change in herself: 'She was no longer wrestling with her grief, but could sit down with it as a lasting companion and make it a sharer in her thoughts.' Some writers have seen grief as a clarifying, and creative, force. Herman Melville suggested that what he called 'grief's wonderful fire' allows us to 'see all things as they are'. Marcel Proust wrote that 'Happiness alone is beneficial for the body, but it is grief that develops the powers of the mind.' Many might feel that intellectual development at this price could be too dearly bought, and against the suggestion the words of the Queen Mother after the death of George VI have a disarming simplicity: 'How small and selfish is sorrow. But it bangs one about until one is senseless.'

They that mourn shall be comforted.
– THE BIBLE

If we had no winter, the spring would not be so pleasant; if we did not sometimes taste of adversity, prosperity would not be so welcome.
– ANNE BRADSTREET

Grief is itself a medicine.
– WILLIAM COWPER

They are the silent griefs which cut the heart-strings.
– JOHN FORD

When one door of happiness closes, another opens; but often we look so long at the closed door that we do not see the one that has been opened for us.
– HELEN KELLER

Grief is one of the things that has the power to silence us. It is a whisper in the world and a clamour within.
– ANNA QUINDLEN

* * *

Happiness

see also Grief

Happiness is, according to a much-modified slogan of the mid twentieth century, anything from a warm puppy to a cigar called Hamlet. Earlier writers have given similarly diverse views that are not always particularly encouraging. A character in one of Dryden's plays thought that the only happiness we could expect was not so much pleasure as 'rest from pain'. In classical Greece, the Athenian statesman Solon thought that until someone was safely dead, they should be called 'lucky' rather than 'happy'. And even if happiness is attained and recognized, the results may not be what we could hope. 'A lifetime of happiness! No man alive could bear it: it would be hell on earth,' said Tanner in George Bernard Shaw's *Man and Superman*.

Tanner would have been alarmed by the approach of a character in Evelyn Waugh's *Decline and Fall*, who would probably have asked for nothing better than a lifetime of happiness: 'When you've been in the soup as often as I have, it gives you a sort of feeling that everything's for the best ... I don't believe one can ever be unhappy for long provided one does just exactly what one wants.' However, even a determined pursuit of pleasure may not be the answer, as a rueful comment by Mickey Rooney suggests: 'Had I been brighter, the ladies been gentler, the Scotch been weaker, had the gods been kinder, had the dice been hotter, this could have been a one-sentence story: Once upon a time I lived happily ever after.'

Happiness sneaks in through a door you didn't know you'd left open.
– JOHN BARRYMORE

Happiness is good health – and a bad memory.
– INGRID BERGMAN

It was roses, roses, all the way.
– ROBERT BROWNING

If merely 'feeling good' could decide, drunkenness would be the supremely valid human experience.
– WILLIAM JAMES

Happiness is nonetheless true happiness because it must come to an end, nor do thought and love lose their value because they are not everlasting.
– BERTRAND RUSSELL

True happiness comes from the joy of deeds well done, the zest of creating things new.
– ANTOINE DE SAINT-EXUPÉRY

* * *

Health

see also Diets

'It is not to live but to be healthy that makes a life,' said the Roman poet Martial. However, the maintenance of a satisfactory state of health is often associated with considerable effort. In the early eighteenth century, Jonathan Swift remarked in a personal letter to the Archbishop of Dublin, 'I row after health like a waterman, and ride after it like a postboy.' He might have been looking forward to the world of two centuries later, when Robertson Davies noted that 'Not to be healthy ... is one of the few sins that modern society is willing to recognize or condemn.'

Different people have had their own recipes for a healthy life. Sydney Smith was sure that digestion was 'the great secret of life'. The humorist Stephen Leacock wrote, 'Get your room full of good air, then shut up the windows and keep it. It will keep for years. Anyway, don't keep using your lungs all the time. Let them rest.' Jennifer Paterson, noting that at the age of seventy she was 'in fine fettle', attributed this to her personal regime of 'Lots of meat, drink and cigarettes and not giving in to things'.

Sometimes, of course, health has to be reached by a difficult route. 'Going cold turkey,' noted Homer Simpson, 'isn't as delicious as it sounds.' Even here, however, there may be some comfort. Keith Richards is quoted as saying encouragingly, 'Cold turkey is not so bad after you've done it ten or twelve times.'

If I'd known I was gonna live this long, I'd have taken better care of myself.
– EUBIE BLAKE
(at the age of one hundred)

Health consists of having the same diseases as one's neighbours.
– QUENTIN CRISP

My idea of exercise is a good, brisk sit.
– PHYLLIS DILLER

The average, healthy, well-adjusted adult gets up at seven-thirty in the morning feeling just plain terrible.
– JEAN KERR

Here I am, dying of a hundred good symptoms.
– ALEXANDER POPE

Use your health, even to the point of wearing it out. That is what it is for.
– GEORGE BERNARD SHAW

* * *

Home

see also Gardens, Hospitality

Home, according to the proverb, is where the heart is, but there have been other definitions. The American poet Robert Frost said it was 'the place where, when you have to go there, they have to take you in'. Helen Rowland said home was 'any four walls that enclose the right person'.

William Cowper wrote of 'Fireside enjoyments, home-born happiness', and George and Weedon Grossmith's Mr Pooter enquired, 'What's the good of a home when you are never in it?' However, not everyone has felt the same. George Bernard Shaw thought that the great advantage of a hotel was that it was 'a refuge from home life'.

Home life may offer a variety of comforts. In the seventeenth century, Samuel Pepys recorded a decidedly unluxurious scene: 'Home, and, being washing-day, dined upon cold meat.' D. H. Lawrence, in more recent times, saw possibilities in looking after yourself: 'I got the blues thinking of the future, so I left off and made some marmalade. It's amazing how it cheers one up to shred oranges and scrub floors.'

William Morris recommended, 'Have nothing in your houses that you do not know to be useful, or believe to be beautiful', but not everyone can rise to this injunction. Herbert Beerbohm Tree commented sardonically that 'The national sport of England is obstacle-racing. People fill their rooms with useless and cumbersome furniture, and spend the rest of their lives trying to dodge it.'

You can never go home again, but the truth is you can never leave home, so it's all right.
– MAYA ANGELOU

The best time for planning a book is while you're doing the dishes.
– AGATHA CHRISTIE

There was no need to do any housework at all. After the first four years the dirt doesn't get any worse.
– QUENTIN CRISP

And though home is a name, a word, it is a strong one; stronger than magician ever spoke, or spirit answered to.
– CHARLES DICKENS

She viewed ethnic cleansing, famine and genocide as direct threats to her furniture.
– ARUNDHATI ROY

Home is a place not only of strong affections, but of entire unreserve; it is life's undress rehearsal, its back-room, its dressing-room.
– HARRIET BEECHER STOWE

* * *

Honesty

Honesty may, as the proverb says, be the best policy; it has often been seen as a somewhat dangerous commodity. In the sixteenth century, the French essayist and moralist Michel de Montaigne wrote, 'I speak truth, not so much as I would, but as much as I dare.' Across the centuries, he would have recognized the grim humour in a comment attributed to Groucho Marx: 'These are my principles. If you don't like them, I have others.' A character in John Dryden's *Amphitryon*, resolving to 'lie abominably', reflected, 'I never saw any good that came of telling truth.' A different point of view, however, comes from William Blake: 'Always be ready to speak your mind, and a base man will avoid you.'

There are different ways to measure honesty. The Australian writer Lennie Lower recommended a practical approach: 'The best way to tell gold is to pass the nugget around a crowded bar, and ask them if it's gold. If it comes back, it's not gold.' Two centuries before, Sir Walter Scott had threatened his servant with an epitaph which would have displayed the man's qualified approach to 'absolute truth': 'Here lies one who might have been trusted with untold gold, but not with unmeasured whisky.' Such behaviour would have shocked John Ruskin, who provided a ringing endorsement of honesty: 'Your honesty is *not* to be based either on religion or policy. Both your religion and policy must be based on it. Your honesty must be based, as the sun is, in vacant heaven; poised, as the lights in the firmament, which have rule over the day and over the night.' He would probably not have seen the humour in the American satirist Stephen Colbert's coinage of the word 'truthiness' to define 'Truth that comes from the gut, not books.'

I am one of the few honest men that I have ever known.
– F. SCOTT FITZGERALD

No man, for any considerable period, can wear one face to himself and another to the multitude without finally getting bewildered as to which may be true.
– NATHANIEL HAWTHORNE

In an autobiography one cannot avoid writing 'often' where truth would require that 'once' be written.
– FRANZ KAFKA

Honesty has come to mean the privilege of insulting you to your face without expecting redress.
– JUDITH MARTIN

Who ever knew Truth put to the worse, in a free and open encounter.
– JOHN MILTON

Everyone is entitled to their own opinions, but not their own facts.
– DANIEL PATRICK MOYNIHAN

Though I am not naturally honest, I am so sometimes by chance.
– WILLIAM SHAKESPEARE
(self-assessment by Autolycus, the 'snapper-up of
  unconsidered trifles' in *The Winter's Tale*)

* * *

Hope

'Hope', according to Alexander Pope, 'springs eternal in the human breast.' While few would deny this, there are varying views as to whether it is a good thing. In the sixteenth century, Francis Bacon wrote that 'Hope is a good breakfast, but it is a bad supper.' Two centuries later, picking up the metaphor, Benjamin Franklin said, 'He that lives upon hope will die fasting.' He might have understood the sentiment of the notice reported to be posted in John Osborne's bathroom, 'Since I gave up hope I feel much better.' In our own time, the crime writer Sara Paretsky has dismissed the tantalizing properties of hope, explaining why she is a pessimist: 'Some people say, the glass is half empty, some say it is half full. I say: "I didn't even get a glass!"'

Proverbially, 'Hope deferred maketh the heart sick.' The implication is that in the end hope must be satisfied to be worthwhile, but a different point of view is suggested in Robert Louis Stevenson's famous maxim, 'It is better to travel hopefully than to arrive.' And hope, as has been seen, is a nat-

ural force – which may explain the rather gloomy comment
of Dr Johnson, on hearing that an acquaintance had remar-
ried. As Boswell recounted the story, 'A gentleman who had
been very unhappy in marriage married almost immediately
after his wife died. Dr Johnson said, it was the triumph of
hope over experience.'

**One of the things I learned the hard way was that it
doesn't pay to get discouraged. Keeping busy and making
optimism a way of life can restore your faith in yourself.**
– LUCILLE BALL

**Hope is the power of being cheerful in circumstances we
know to be desperate.**
– G. K. CHESTERTON

Westward, look, the land is bright.
– ARTHUR HUGH CLOUGH

**In the night of death, hope sees a star, and listening love
can hear the rustle of a wing.**
– ROBERT GREEN INGERSOLL

**Hope is the feeling you have that the feeling you have
isn't permanent.**
– JEAN KERR

Where there's life there's hope.
– TERENCE

Horses

see also **Leisure, Sport**

Horses are often treasured by their owners. The Roman Emperor Caligula went so far to appoint his to an official position, which in nineteenth-century America provided a figure of speech for the bitter-tongued John Randolph of Roanoke. Condemning an appointment made by John Quincy Adams when President, he said, 'Never were abilities so much below mediocrity so well rewarded; no, not when Caligula's horse was made Consul.'

In *Hillingdon Hall* (1845) by Robert Surtees, Mrs Flather attempted to borrow a horse from Mr Jorrocks so that her servant could go over to Sellborough to get a prescription made up. However, her assurances that 'He is a very careful rider, and will take great care of it' are met with an absolute refusal from principle. Mr Jorrock's letter of reply began: 'Dear Mrs F., Three things I never lends – my 'oss, my wife, and my name.'

Accounts of the Duke of Wellington often include a description of his charger Copenhagen, clearly an animal of character. The writer William Hamilton Maxwell in his *Life of Field-Marshal his Grace the Duke of Wellington* (1839–41) wrote, 'On the memorable day of Waterloo, though the great captain had been on his back for eighteen hours, Copenhagen gave little sign of being beat, for on the Duke patting him on the quarter, as he dismounted after the battle, the game little horse struck out as playfully as if he had only had an hour's ride in the park.' (Other commentators have described what happened more succinctly as Copenhagen's lashing out with a narrow miss on the Field-Marshal's skull.) No malice, however was borne: Copenhagen was to die at 'an illustrious old age' at Strathfieldsay, where 'The Duke rarely omitted to visit him, and the ladies of the family made him an especial pet.'

One was presented with a small, hairy individual and, out of general curiosity, one climbed on.
– ANNE, PRINCESS ROYAL

A canter is the cure for every evil.
– BENJAMIN DISRAELI

Where in this wide world can a person find nobility without pride, friendship without envy, or beauty without vanity? Here, where grace is laced with muscle and strength by gentleness confined.
– RONALD DUNCAN

A horse is dangerous at both ends and uncomfortable in the middle.
– IAN FLEMING

They say princes learn no art truly, but the art of horsemanship. The reason is, the brave beast is no flatterer. He will throw a prince as soon as his groom.
– BEN JONSON

Eclipse first – the rest nowhere.
– DENNIS O'KELLY
(of a famous racehorse, grandfather of Wellington's charger
 Copenhagen)

A leg at each corner.
– NORMAN THELWELL
(title of Thelwell's 'complete guide to equitation')

* * *

Hospitality

see also Food, Home

'Mankind,' said the critic Max Beerbohm, 'is divisible into
two great classes, hosts and guests.' The responsibility of
being the host can weigh heavily. Lady Gregory, the Anglo-
Irish chatelaine who was the friend and patron of W. B. Yeats,
once wrote (perhaps after a particularly exhausting house-
party), 'I am so tired of housekeeping I dreamed I was being
served up for my guests and awoke only when the knife was
at my throat.' In the twentieth century, Walter Sickert is said
to have told Denton Welch, 'Come again when you can't stay
so long.'

The balance of the party may be of particular concern.
William King in the early eighteenth century gave explicit
directions as to numbers: 'Crowd not your table: let your
numbers be Not more than seven, and never less than three.'

Lord Macaulay, on the other hand, seems to have been less interested in the number of his guests than in the precautions necessary to guard against their potential dishonesty, alluding in one line to 'Ye diners-out from whom we guard our spoons'. (A similar sentiment probably informed Ralph Waldo Emerson's comment, 'The louder he talked of his honour, the faster we counted our spoons.')

Some comments come from the point of view of the prospective guest. Jonathan Swift evoked one who was more interested in conversation and company than food: 'He showed me his bill of fare to tempt me to dine with him; Poh, said I, I value not your bill of fare; give me your bill of company.'

The guest whose tardiness delays the meal should have the dining-room door slammed in his face.
– ANTONIN CARÊME

Only if you want to eat quickly eat *chez moi.*
– NAPOLEON

Strange to see how a good dinner and feasting reconciles everybody.
– SAMUEL PEPYS

A free-loader is a confirmed guest. He is the man who is always willing to come to dinner.
– DAMON RUNYON

I always feel that I have two duties to perform with a parting guest: one, to see that he doesn't forget anything that is his; the other, to see that he doesn't take anything that is mine.
– ALFRED NORTH WHITEHEAD

* * *

Humour

'We are not amused,' Queen Victoria is supposed to have said, and inevitably what is funny to one person is often quite unfunny to another. This can lead to difficulties: as George Eliot wrote, 'A difference of taste in jokes is a great strain on the affections.' The American humorist Will Rogers, however, has suggested one possibility of finding common ground: 'Everything is funny as long as it is happening to someone else.'

Sigmund Freud thought that a good joke opened the door to relief and elation – leading in time to Ken Dodd's riposte that 'The trouble with Freud is that he never had to play the old Glasgow Empire on a Saturday night after Rangers and Celtic had both lost.'

Laughter is seen as both essential and dangerous. The essayist Joseph Addison wrote in the eighteenth century that 'If we may believe our logicians, man is distinguished from all other creatures by the faculty of laughter.' His near contemporary, Lord Chesterfield, however, warned his son,

'In my mind, there is nothing so illiberal and so ill-bred, as audible laughter', adding rather alarmingly that 'since I have had the full use of my reason, nobody has ever heard me laugh'. It is something of a relief to turn to another figure of the eighteenth century, Nicolas de Chamfort, and find his assertion that 'The most wasted of all days is the day one did not laugh.'

It is a good deed to forget a poor joke.
– BRENDAN BRACKEN

Ah well, perhaps one has to be very old before one learns how to be amused rather than shocked.
– PEARL S. BUCK

There's terrific merit in having no sense of humour, no sense of irony, practically no sense of anything at all. If you are born with these so-called defects you have a very good chance of getting to the top.
– PETER COOK

Comedy is medicine.
– TREVOR GRIFFITHS

People who have not got a sense of humour should not be put in charge.
– ROBERT RUNCIE

Anything said off the cuff has usually been written on it first.
– ROBIN SKELTON

* * *

Ideas

see also Innovation, Intelligence, Thought

In the eighteenth century, Voltaire wrote that 'One can resist the invasion of an army; but one cannot resist the invasion of ideas.' This could be seen in a positive light, as setting individual enterprise against totalitarianism, but in the twentieth century another French philosopher, Alain, warned against fanaticism: 'Nothing is more dangerous than an idea, when you have only one idea.' And even if things are not taken to such extremes, there may be drawbacks. The American journalist and critic H. L. Mencken commented wryly, 'A society made up of individuals who were all capable of original thought would probably be unendurable. The pressure of ideas would simply drive it frantic.'

The American jurist Oliver Wendell Holmes, Jr, thought that the key point was that ideas should be shared: 'Many ideas grow better when transplanted into another mind than in the one where they sprang up.' However, not everyone is likely to be receptive. In the nineteenth century, the constitutionalist Walter Bagehot thought that 'One of the greatest pains to human nature is the pain of a new idea.' A century later, the scientist Peter Medawar used an image from his own intellectual world to illustrate a negative reaction to such pain: 'The human mind treats a new idea the way the body treats a strange protein – it rejects it.'

It is something of a relief, after this, to turn to the assertion by Don Juan in George Bernard Shaw's 1903 play *Man and Superman* that 'This creature Man, who in his own selfish affairs is a coward to the backbone, will fight for an idea like a hero.'

Imagination is the highest kite that one can fly.
– LAUREN BACALL

Stung by the splendour of a sudden thought.
– ROBERT BROWNING

All revolutionary new ideas ... pass through three stages, which may be summed up by these reactions: 1. 'It's crazy – don't waste my time'; 2. 'It's possible, but it's not worth doing'; and 3. 'I always said it was a good idea.'
– ARTHUR C. CLARKE

An original idea. That can't be too hard. The library must be full of them.
– STEPHEN FRY

When an idea is dead it is embalmed in a textbook.
– PATRICK GEDDES

Everyone is in love with his own ideas.
– CARL JUNG

An idea isn't responsible for the people who believe in it.
– DON MARQUIS

* * *

Idleness

see also Leisure, Work

Lord Chesterfield called idleness 'the refuge of weak minds, and the holiday of fools'. To others, however, idleness may be welcome or unwelcome, depending on whether the state has been chosen or enforced. Beau Brummel, the Regency leader of fashion, clearly preferred to take things at his own pace, commenting that 'I always like to have the morning well-aired before I get up.' The nineteenth-century American humorist Artemus Ward was explicit about his preference: 'I am happiest when I am idle. I could live for months without performing any labour, and at the expiration of that time I should feel fresh and vigorous enough to go right on in the same way for numerous more months.'

The point here, of course, is that both Brummel and Ward had chosen to be idle. As Jerome K. Jerome wrote in 1886 in his *Idle Thoughts of an Idle Fellow*, 'It is impossible to enjoy idling thoroughly unless one has plenty of work to do.' And the harsh position of someone who is idle not through choice was laid out by the New Zealand writer Charles Orwell Brasch. Looking back to being unemployed in 1938 Dunedin, he wrote, 'It is not only an offence against society to be seen in the streets flaunting the fact that one does not work like everyone else; it challenges the settled order of things ... It makes one an object of suspicion, and more, an enemy.'

Brasch conjured up a grim reality that is a world away from James Thurber's insouciant reworking of a famous line: 'It is better to have loafed and lost than never to have loafed at all.'

Of course I don't look busy. I did it right the first time.
– SCOTT ADAMS

What a terrible burden it is to have nothing to do!
– NICOLAS BOILEAU-DESPRÉAUX

We owe most of our great inventions and most of the achievements of genius to idleness – either enforced or voluntary.
– AGATHA CHRISTIE

How various his employments, whom the world Calls idle.
– WILLIAM COWPER

It was such a lovely day I thought it was a pity to get up.
– W. SOMERSET MAUGHAM

It is in our idleness, in our dreams, that the submerged truth sometimes comes to the top.
– VIRGINIA WOOLF

* * *

Innovation

see also Business, Change, Ideas, Progress

The Bible warns us against putting 'new wine into old bottles', and the process of innovation has often been seen as a risky one – although Clement Attlee thought that as a people we had a particular advantage: 'I think the British have the distinction above all other nations of being able to put new wine into old bottles without bursting them.' The necessity of experiencing what the art historian Ian Dunlop called 'the shock of the new' is generally recognized, since the alternative would be the path sardonically indicated by Max Beerbohm: 'Anything that is worth doing has been done frequently. Things hitherto undone should be given, I suspect, a wide berth.'

A serious application of Beerbohm's principle would lead to what the Scottish philosopher and historian James Mackintosh described as a state of 'masterly inactivity'. A quite different point of view comes from a much earlier period, in a saying attributed to Lao Tzu, the founder of Taoism: 'A journey of a thousand miles begins with a single step.' In the sixteenth century, Francis Bacon warned that 'He that will not apply new remedies must expect new evils, for time is the greatest innovator.' Nearer to modern times, the American inventor and businessman Thomas Alva Edison once told an interviewer, 'Some day some fellow will invent a way of concentrating and storing up sunshine to use instead of this old, absurd Prometheus scheme of fire. I'll do the trick myself if someone else doesn't get at it.'

Edison gives voice to the restless creativity of the innovator, and in today's world Steve Jobs also stresses the importance of the individual. 'Innovation has nothing to do with how many R&D dollars you have. ...It's about the people you have.'

A fool ... is a man who never tried an experiment in his life.
– ERASMUS DARWIN

Innovation is the specific instrument of entrepeneurship. The act that endows resources with a new capacity to create wealth.
– PETER DRUCKER

The difficulty lies, not in the new ideas, but in escaping from the old ones, which ramify ... into every corner of our minds.
– JOHN MAYNARD KEYNES

Whatever has happened in my quest for innovation has been part of my quest for immaculate reality.
– GEORGE LUCAS

Nobody ever talks of entrepeneurship as survival, but that's exactly what it is and what nurtures creative thinking.
– ANITA RODDICK

Discovery consists of seeing what everybody has seen and thinking what nobody has thought.
– ALBERT VON SZENT-GYÖRGI

* * *

Intelligence

see also Ideas, Thought

'I am a brain, Watson. The rest of me is a mere appendix,' said Sherlock Holmes to his friend in one of Conan Doyle's stories. He would presumably have claimed to have both intelligence and ability according to the definition provided by the philosopher Alfred North Whitehead: 'Intelligence is quickness to apprehend as distinct from ability, which is the capacity to act wisely on the thing apprehended.' For both of them, the ability to reason at speed was crucial; the opposite of the laborious thought processes of Gonzalo in Shakespeare's *The Tempest*, of whom Sebastian said mockingly, 'Look, he's winding up the watch of his wit, By and by it will strike.'

Some people (unlike Sherlock Holmes) do not wish to demonstrate their abilities too publicly; in the seventeenth century La Rochefoucauld thought that 'The height of cleverness is to be able to conceal it.' However, it may be difficult to do this when encountering another intelligent person. As Blaise Pascal wrote in the same century, 'The more intelligence one has the more people one finds original. Commonplace people see no difference between men.'

Intelligence is often linked with a practical approach, and common sense, but there are warnings here too. The French philosopher René Descartes wrote wryly, 'Common sense is the best distributed thing in the world, for we all think we possess a good share of it.' And even if we are right in our supposition, there are dangers; according to Albert Einstein, 'Common sense is the collection of prejudices acquired by the age of eighteen.'

My brain: it's my second favourite organ.
– WOODY ALLEN

I'm not very clever, but I'm quite intelligent.
– DIRK BOGARDE

The test of a first-rate intelligence is the ability to hold two opposed ideas in the mind at the same time, and still retain the ability to function.
– F. SCOTT FITZGERALD

A highbrow is the kind of person who looks at a sausage and thinks of Picasso.
– A. P. HERBERT

She is a smart old broad. It is a pity she is so nefarious.
– DAMON RUNYON

The mind is also an erogenous zone.
– RAQUEL WELCH

* * *

Jewellery

see also **Appearance**

In George Eliot's poem *The Spanish Gypsy*, a character said of a ruby earring, 'These gems have life in them: their colours speak, Say what words fail of.' Different gemstones are often taken as the perfect example of a particular colour. Rebecca in Scott's *Ivanhoe* had teeth 'as white as pearl'. In Shakespeare's play, Romeo's first love Rosaline was noted for her 'ruby lips'. Tennyson, evoking land and sea, wrote that 'A livelier emerald twinkles in the grass, A purer sapphire melts into the sea.'

Most quotations about jewellery, however, reflect the value as well as the beauty of precious stones. 'Diamonds', ran the song, 'are a girl's best friend', and there is plenty of literary precedent for the belief. In Ben Jonson's play, the lustful Volpone tried to tempt Celia with a diamond which he told her would have 'bought' the Roman Empress Lollia Paulina 'When she came in like starlight, hid with jewels That were the spoils of provinces'. Celia resisted Volpone's

141

lure; he might have found a different reaction from a twenti-eth-century figure. The actress Zsa-Zsa Gabor is quoted as say-ing reflectively, 'I never hated a man enough to give him his diamonds back.' A comment that perhaps finds an echo in an exchange in one of Mae West's films: '"Goodness, what beau-tiful diamonds!" "Goodness had nothing to do with it."'

The gold-digging Lorelei Lee of *Gentleman Prefer Blondes* reflected philosophically that 'Kissing your hand may make you feel very very good but a diamond and safire bracelet lasts for ever.' She would have applauded Richard Burton's gift to Elizabeth Taylor of a diamond which he said had 'A carat fig-ure large enough to make a turnip'.

It's tacky to wear diamonds before you're forty; and even that's risky. They only look right on the really old girls.
– TRUMAN CAPOTE
(Holly Golightly's view in *Breakfast at Tiffany's*)

Never wear artistic jewellery; it ruins a woman's reputation.
– COLETTE

It was not a bosom to repose upon, but it was a capital bosom to hang jewels upon.
– CHARLES DICKENS

I had very good dentures once. Some magnificent gold work. It's the only form of jewellery a man can wear that women fully appreciate.
– GRAHAM GREENE

Those in the cheaper seats clap. The rest of you rattle your jewellery.
– JOHN LENNON

I prefer liberty to chains of diamonds.
– LADY MARY WORTLEY MONTAGU

Let us not be too particular. It is better to have old second-hand diamonds than none at all.
– MARK TWAIN

* * *

Journalism

see also Writing

The eighteenth-century novelist Henry Fielding commented sardonically that a newspaper 'consisted of just the same number of words, whether there be any news in it or not', and later voices have also questioned the value of a reporter's work. In one of G. K. Chesterton's Father Brown stories, a journalist admits that 'Journalism largely consists in saying "Lord Jones Dead" to people who never knew that Lord Jones was alive.' Severer criticism is indicated by Humbert Wolfe's poem 'Over the Fire'. Having thanked God that it was impossible to 'bribe or twist' the British journalist, the poet concluded that in view of what such a man was prepared to do 'unbribed, There's no occasion to'. This appears to be in line with a comment attributed to the British journalist Nicholas Tomalin: 'The only qualities essential for success in journalism are ratlike cunning, a plausible manner, and a little literary ability.'

There are of course more elevated views of life in 'the Fourth Estate'. According to the French writer Marguerite Duras, 'Journalism without a moral position is impossible. Every journalist is a moralist.' She would have understood the opinion expressed by the American dramatist Arthur Miller, 'A good newspaper, I suppose, is a nation talking to itself.'

The power of the press was noted, with exasperation, by Stanley Baldwin. Considering the political standpoint of the proprietor Lord Beaverbrook in relation to the *Daily Express*, the Prime Minister borrowed a phrase from his cousin Rudyard Kipling to speak crushingly of 'Power without responsibility – the prerogative of the harlot throught the ages'. It is however only fair to balance such judgements by considering a journalist's view of politicians. The American Russell Baker described his role as a journalist reporting the Senate as 'Sitting on marble floors, waiting for somebody to come out and lie to me'.

No news is good news, and no journalists is even better.
– NICOLAS BENTLEY

News is the first rough draft of history.
– PHILIP GRAHAM

Were it left to me to decide whether we should have a
government without newspapers, or newspapers without
a government, I should not hesitate for a moment to
prefer the latter.
– THOMAS JEFFERSON

Accuracy, accuracy, accuracy.
– JOSEPH PULITZER
(key requirement for his reporters)

Comment is free, but facts are sacred.
– C. P. SCOTT

Rock journalism is people who can't write interviewing
people who can't talk for people who can't read.
– FRANK ZAPPA

* * *

Knowledge

see also Education, Science

'All men naturally desire knowledge,' said the philosopher
Aristotle. Such desire may or may not be disinterested; a
phrase from Francis Bacon which has become proverbial is
often used to suggest a particular motive for the acquisition
of knowledge: 'For knowledge itself is power.' In the twentieth century, the American writer Ethel Mumford gave

Bacon's words a further twist: 'Knowledge is power if you know it about the right person.'

Sherlock Holmes, a figure noted for his wide knowledge, once told Dr Watson that there was no point in trying to keep everything in one's mind. 'A man should keep his little brain attic stocked with all the furniture that he is likely to use, and the rest he can put away in the lumber-room of his library, where he can get it if he wants it.' (At this point in the story, he asked Watson to hand him down 'the letter K of the American Encyclopaedia', where he found the necessary information about the Ku Klux Klan.) Holmes would probably have sympathized with the disapproving comment of the philosopher and broadcaster C. E. M. Joad in the 1950s, 'There was never an age in which useless knowledge was more important than in ours.'

Even useful knowledge should not necessarily be displayed to others. Lord Chesterfield warned his son, 'Wear your learning, like your watch, in a private pocket: and do not pull it out and strike it; merely to show that you have one. If you are asked what o'clock it is, tell it; but do not proclaim it hourly and unasked like the watchman.'

They know enough who know how to learn.
– HENRY ADAMS

I prefer tongue-tied knowledge to ignorant loquacity.
– CICERO

Try to learn something about everything, and everything about something.
– THOMAS HENRY HUXLEY

My experience is what I agree to attend to.
– WILLIAM JAMES

That is what learning is. You suddenly understand something you've understood all your life, but in a new way.
– DORIS LESSING

The desire of knowledge, like the thirst of riches, increases ever with the acquisition of it.
– LAURENCE STERNE

* * *

Language

see also Conversation, Writing

'Language', said Dr Johnson, 'is the dress of thought.' The American poet Walt Whitman would have agreed, but went into much more detail: 'Language ... is not an abstract construction of the learned, or of dictionary-makers but is something arising out of the work, needs, ties, joys, affections, tastes, of long generations of humanity, and has its bases broad and low, close to the ground.' Or as Lily Tomlin, less seriously, put it, 'Man invented language in order to satisfy his deep need to complain.' (Some complaints, inevitably, arise from our encountering someone who does not agree with our own view of language. In 1947 Raymond Chandler wrote to his publisher, 'Would you convey my compliments to the purist who reads your proofs and tell him or her that I write in a sort of broken-down patois which is something like the way a Swiss waiter talks, and that when I split an infinitive, God damn it, I split it so it will stay split.')

Language is a powerful tool. The American journalist Edward R. Murrow, considering Winston Churchill as a war leader, wrote, 'He mobilized the English language and sent it into battle to steady his fellow countrymen and hearten those Europeans upon whom the long dark night of tyranny had descended.'

English is of course only one of many world languages – a thought which presumably would have given pleasure to Johnson, since he told Boswell, 'I am always sorry when any language is lost, because languages are the pedigree of nations.' He would have disapproved of the simple view of the lady at the court of Versailles who (according to Voltaire) said regretfully, 'What a great pity it is that the adventure at the tower of Babel should have produced the confusion of languages; if it weren't for that, everyone would always have spoken French.'

Language is fossil poetry.
– RALPH WALDO EMERSON

Whoever is not acquainted with foreign languages knows nothing of his own.
– GOETHE

Thanks to words we have been able to rise above the brutes, and thanks to words, we have often sunk to the level of demons.
– ALDOUS HUXLEY

In his whole life man achieves nothing so great and so wonderful as what he achieved when he learned to talk.
– OTTO JESPERSEN

Language tethers us to the world; without it we spin like atoms.
– PENELOPE LIVELY

You know, she speaks eighteen languages. And she can't say 'No' in any of them.
– DOROTHY PARKER

In certain trying circumstances, urgent circumstances, desperate circumstances, profanity furnishes a relief denied even to prayer.
– MARK TWAIN

* * *

Law

While not everyone would agree with Charles Dickens's Mr Bumble that 'the law is a ass – a idiot', it is not difficult to find critical comments. In the classical world, the Athenian statesman Solon saw the limitation of a legal system: 'Laws are like spiders' webs, which hold firm when any light, yielding object falls upon them, while a larger thing breaks through them and escapes.' Centuries later, Jonathan Swift used a similar image: 'Laws are like cobwebs, which may catch small flies, but let wasps and hornets break through.'

It is not only strength or weight which allow safe engagement with law. The seventeenth-century judge Sir John Maynard thought that knowledge was also essential: 'Laws are edged tools; those that understand them, make good use of them; and those that do not understand them, will find that they are sharp, and will cut.' And the German writer Johann Wolfgang von Goethe saw another benefit to familiarizing yourself with the intricacies of the law: 'If one were to study all the laws, one would have absolutely no time to break them.' Someone in that position would not find themselves at the mercy of the savage Scottish judge of the eighteenth century, Lord Braxfield, who said threateningly, 'Let them bring me prisoners, and I'll find them law.'

One solution might be to choose the law as a profession, this too has occasioned adverse comment. In Boswell's *Life of*

Samuel Johnson we are told, 'Johnson observed, that "he did not care to speak ill of any man behind his back, but he believed the gentleman was an attorney".'

In the end, however, the law is an essential defence for any society. As John Locke wrote in the seventeenth century, 'Wherever Law ends, Tyranny begins.' Or as the barrister Helena Kennedy has said in our own time, 'The law is the bedrock of a nation. It tells us who we are, what we value, who has power and who hasn't.'

Laws are like sausages. It's better not to see them being made.
– OTTO VON BISMARCK

Trial by jury ... is the lamp that shows that freedom lives.
– LORD DEVLIN

A jury consists of twelve persons chosen to decide who has the better lawyer.
– ROBERT FROST

I have come to regard the law courts not as a cathedral but rather as a casino.
– RICHARD INGRAMS

No brilliance is needed in the law. Nothing but common sense, and relatively clean finger nails.
– JOHN MORTIMER

A lawyer with his briefcase can steal more than a thousand men with guns.
– Mario Puzo

* * *

Leisure

see also Idleness, Work

Leisure is not the same as idleness. It represents not so much the cessation of work, as the opportunity to expend one's mental and physical abilities on some enjoyable activity. Thomas Hood's oppressed seamstress in 'The Song of the Shirt' did not have this luxury; in her world of 'Stitch, stitch, stitch' there was 'No blessed leisure for Love or Hope'. A different kind of pressure is reflected in the comment of the harried Jane Welsh Carlyle, 'They must be comfortable people who have leisure to think about going to heaven! My most constant and pressing anxiety is to keep out of bedlam, that's all ...'

Hood's seamstress epitomizes desperate poverty; a world away from the life of Jane Austen's Mr Bennett in *Pride and Prejudice*. Having learned of the engagements of his two elder daughters, he is able to relax in his library, telling Elizabeth, 'If any young men come for Mary or Kitty, send them in, for I am quite at leisure.'

Proper use of leisure is often associated with improvement. Samuel Johnson thought that 'All intellectual improvement arises from leisure.' Disraeli, looking from the individual to the whole of society, said sweepingly, 'Increased means and increased leisure are the two civilizers of man.' In fact, as Shaw pointed out, leisure may not be a wholly welcome responsibility: 'The secret of being miserable is to have leisure to bother about whether you are happy or not. The cure for it is occupation.'

Never be afraid to sit awhile, and think.
– LORRAINE HANSBERRY

Leisure is the mother of philosophy.
– THOMAS HOBBES

They talk of the *dignity of work.* **Bosh ... The dignity is in leisure.**
– HERMAN MELVILLE

Now the end, I take it, is all one, to live at more leisure and at one's ease.
– MONTAIGNE

The insupportable labour of doing nothing.
– RICHARD STEELE

To be able to fill leisure intelligently is the last product of civilization.
– ARNOLD TOYNBEE

* * *

Life

see also **Career, Death**

Life has been variously declared to be 'a bowl of cherries', 'one damned thing after another', 'mostly froth and bubble', and 'not all beer and skittles', and there has been no shortage of other comments. Some of them, of course, express regret. 'If life had a second edition, how I would correct the proofs,' said the troubled eighteenth-century poet John Clare. A century later George Borrow commented, 'Youth will be served, every dog has his day, and mine has been a fine one.'

Richard Dawkins, writing that 'The essence of life is statistical improbability on a colossal scale', was concerned with the nature of life itself, but others have been less concerned with its essential nature than with how it should be lived. The travel writer and novelist Gerald Brenan thought that 'We should live as if we were going to live forever, yet at the back of our minds remember that our time is short.' The Canadian novelist Margaret Atwood has said crisply, 'If you're not annoying somebody, you're not really alive.'

The Australian Prime Minister Malcolm Fraser once told an audience that 'Life is not meant to be easy.' He was quoting a character in one of Shaw's plays, who advised, 'Life is not meant to be easy, my child; but take courage, it can be delightful.' Both Fraser and Shaw would have understood the assertion of Polly Adler, 'I am one of those people who just can't help getting a kick out of life – even when it's a kick in the teeth.'

It began in mystery and it will end in mystery, but what a savage and beautiful country lies in between.
– DIANE ACKERMAN

What a wonderful life I've had! I only wish I'd realized it sooner.
– COLETTE

Although the world is full of suffering, it is also full of the overcoming of it.
– HELEN KELLER

Life is what happens to you when you're busy making other plans.
– JOHN LENNON

The proper function of man is to live, not to exist. I shall not waste my days in trying to prolong them. I shall use my time.
– JACK LONDON

Give us the luxuries of life, and we will dispense with its necessities.
– JOHN LOTHROP MOTLEY

All the things I really like to do are either immoral, illegal, or fattening.
– ALEXANDER WOOLLCOTT

* * *

Love

see also Friendship, Marriage

'Greater love hath no man than this, that a man lay down his life for his friends,' offers biblical authority for the disinterested force of love. In the sixteenth century, the courtier and statesman Francis Bacon saw its dangers: 'They do best who, if they cannot but admit love, yet make it keep quarter; and sever it wholly from their serious affairs and actions of life: for if it check once with business, it troubleth men's fortunes, and maketh men, that they can no ways be true to their own ends.' In the 1960s, the Liberal politician Jeremy Thorpe commented mockingly of Harold Macmillan's sacking seven members of his Cabinet to save his own political skin, 'Greater love hath no man than this, that he lay down his friends for his life.'

'Love', according to the proverb, 'makes the world go round', and for many that would be romantic love. The Roman statesman and philosopher Boethius wrote, 'Who can give a law to lovers? Love is a greater law unto itself.' In Jane Austen's *Persuasion*, Anne Elliott asserted that all the privilege she claimed for her sex was 'that of loving longest, when existence or when hope is gone'.

'How do I love thee? Let me count the ways,' asked the speaker in Elizabeth Barrett Browning's *Sonnets from the Portuguese*, and there are a number of evocations of the pleasures, and the pains, of love. Bell in Congreve's *The Old Bachelor* believed that despite her affectations Belinda must be in love with him: 'In my conscience I believe the baggage loves me, for she never speaks well of me her self, nor suffers anybody else to rail me.' Jerome K. Jerome thought that 'Love is like the measles; we all have to go through it.' The lover in John Donne's poem, however, saw love as central to life rather than a passing affliction: 'I wonder by my troth, what thou, and I, Did, till we loved?'

Each moment of the happy lover's hour is worth an age of dull and common life.
– APHRA BEHN

Love, having no geography, knows no boundaries.
– TRUMAN CAPOTE

If grass can grow through cement, love can find you at every time in your life.
– CHER

When you're loved for your flaws, that's when you really feel safe.
– NICOLE KIDMAN

Only one being is missing, and your whole world is bereft of people.
– ALPHONSE DE LAMARTINE

Love is not looking into one another's eyes but looking together in the same direction.
– ANTOINE DE SAINT-EXUPÉRY

Lovers' quarrels are the renewal of love.
– TERENCE

* * *

Luck

see also Success

Napoleon, when considering a man for promotion to high command, is said to have had one key question to ask: 'Is he lucky?' He would have understood the viewpoint of the character in John Webster's revenge tragedy *The White Devil*, who said, 'And of all axioms this shall win the prize, – 'Tis better to be fortunate than wise.' Such good fortune does not necessarily evoke enthusiasm in those less fortunate. The American writer Anne Tyler has pointed out, 'People always call it luck when you've acted more sensibly than they have.' Tony Parsons commented dryly, 'There are few things in the world more reassuring than an unhappy Lottery winner.'

Sometimes one person's good luck derives from another person's bad luck. A modern saying warns, 'It's the second mouse that gets the cheese.' This was foreshadowed in 1920 by a comment from Franklin Delano Roosevelt, who wrote to a friend, 'I sometimes think we consider too much the good luck of the early bird and not the bad luck of the early worm.'

There is plenty of proverbial wisdom about luck, from the assertion that 'It is better to be born lucky than rich' to the encouragement to perseverance 'Third time lucky'. There are even ways in which to help yourself: 'See a pin and pick it up, all the day you'll have good luck.' (The second line continues ominously, 'See a pin and let it lie, you'll want a pin before you die.') It is of course possible to adopt a better-safe-than-sorry approach with luck-bringing objects. The great Danish nuclear physicist Niels Bohr, questioned as to why he had a horseshoe on his wall, responded, 'Of course I don't believe in it. But I understand that it brings you luck whether you believe in it or not.'

We must believe in luck. For how else can we explain the success of those we don't like?
– JEAN COCTEAU

Believe in fate, but lean forward where fate can see you.
– QUENTIN CRISP

Your luck changes only if it's good.
– OGDEN NASH

Where observation is concerned, chance favours only the prepared mind.
– LOUIS PASTEUR

Fate shuffles the cards and we play.

– ARTHUR SCHOPENHAUER

Fortune brings in some boats that are not steered.

– WILLIAM SHAKESPEARE

* * *

Management

see also **Bureacracy, Business, Careers**

'The best-laid schemes o' mice and men Gang aft agley,' wrote Robert Burns, but for many the key to successful planning lies in effective management. The crucial skills may be found in an unexpected source: according to a saying attributed to Lenin, 'Any cook should be able to run the country.'

Lenin's cook was presumably seen as being able to bring practical abilities to the business of government. A less confident approach to the result of promotion is reflected by what we know as 'the Peter Principle', the statement by Laurence J. Peter that 'In a hierarchy every employee tends to rise to his level of incompetence.' (The hierarchy envisioned by Peter might have benefited from the application of Donald Trump's trademark exclamation, popularized in Britain by Sir Alan Sugar, 'You're fired!') In recent years, *The Office*'s David Brent has become the stereotype of an overpromoted manager, with a delusional view of his own effectiveness:

'You will never have another boss like me. Someone who's basically a chilled-out entertainer.'

Fictional Mafia figures, unsurprisingly, tend to offer a no-nonsense approach to management. In the film *Godfather* III, Michael Corleone recalled his father's advice, 'Keep your friends close, but your enemies closer.' Tony Soprano thought that 'Those who want respect, give respect', but was able if necessary to bring things to an end: 'I genuinely don't think there's anything to gain by keeping him around.'

Every organization has its own style of management – and the person who moves to another system may not always be pleasantly surprised. At the end of his life, the composer and conductor Gustav Mahler was conducting the New York Philharmonic Orchestra, which at that time depended for financial support on a number of wealthy American women. After her husband's death, Alma Mahler wrote trenchantly, 'In Vienna, even the Emperor did not dictate to my husband. But in New York, to his amazement, he had ten women ordering him about like a puppet.'

All management is risk management.
– DOUGLAS BARLOW

When management with a reputation for brilliance tackles a business with a reputation for poor fundamental economics, it is the reputation of the business that remains intact.
– WARREN BUFFETT

So much of what we call management consists in making it difficult for people to work.
– PETER DRUCKER

Management is nothing more than motivating other people.
– LEE IACOCCA

Given the choice between being respected and being held dear I prefer to be respected. Love is unstable: today you are loved, tomorrow you're not. Respect is permanent.
– ANTONIO CARLOS DE MAGELHAES

Great reserve and severity of manners are necessary for the command of those who are older than ourselves.
– NAPOLEON

* * *

Marriage

see also Love, Weddings

Marriage is generally assumed to be a desirable state. Many comments, however, suggest that the married state may have its difficulties, although not everyone would put it as strongly as Lord Byron: 'Though women are angels, yet wedlock's the devil.'

Sometimes the enthusiasm expressed is more practical than romantic, as with the proposal voiced by Charles Dickens's Mr Bumble. Hoping to become Master of the Workhouse, he presses his suit with Mrs Corney, Matron of the institution, with the words, 'What a opportunity for a jining of hearts and housekeepings!' In the previous century, Oliver Goldsmith's Vicar of Wakefield had noted that 'I ... chose my wife as she did her wedding gown, not for a fine glossy surface, but such qualities as would wear well.'

It is often tempting to reach for the witty and cynical ('A sort of friendship recognized by the police' – Robert Louis Stevenson), but down the centuries there is also ample evidence for the happiness of marriage. In the nineteenth century, Sydney Smith used the analogy of a pair of scissors to illustrate its essential nature: 'It resembles a pair of shears, so joined that they cannot be separated; often moving in opposite directions, yet always punishing anyone who comes between them.' The eighteenth-century poet Richard Steele signed a letter to his wife, 'A little in drink, but at all times your faithful husband.' And in 2006, the French writer and philosopher André Gorz wrote to his wife, 'It is now fifty-eight years that we have lived together, and I love you more than ever.'

The heart of marriage is memories.
– BILL COSBY

Marriage is a framework to preserve friendship. It is valuable because it gives much more room to develop than just living together. It provides a base from which a person can work at understanding himself and another person.
– ROBERTSON DAVIES

Husbands are like fires. They go out when unattended.
– ZSA ZSA GABOR

The critical period in matrimony is breakfast-time.
– A. P. HERBERT

I've never had a strict policy on marriage. It's unwise.
– JACK NICHOLSON

Before marriage, a man will lie awake thinking about something you said; after marriage, he'll fall asleep before you finish saying it.
– HELEN ROWLAND

* * *

Meetings

see also Bureaucracy

Meetings do not always run smoothly. Charles Dickens, in The Pickwick Papers, described a meeting of the Brick Lane Branch of the United Grand Junction Ebenezer Temperance

Association, which broke up in disorder after the Chairman had announced, 'It's my opinion, sir, that this meeting is drunk, sir.'

The Duke of Wellington, perhaps unsurprisingly, took a brisk approach to meetings. He is said to have been surprised, as Prime Minister, by his first Cabinet meeting: 'An extraordinary affair. I gave them their orders, and they wanted to stay and discuss them.' He would have understood the critical note sounded by an unidentified senior American diplomat in 1995. As reported by William Safire in the *New York Times*, the comment on the international response to the situation in Bosnia ran, 'The French want to attack, the Americans want to bomb, and the British want to have another meeting.' The British wish as reported here presumably resonated with the comment of the economist John Kenneth Galbraith, 'Meetings are indispensable when you don't want to do anything.'

Inevitably, in today's working world, meetings are a way of life; the phrase 'meetings about meetings' is now a commonplace. Our awareness of this kind of lifestyle might lead us to lend a new interpretation to the reputed last words of the economist Adam Smith, who died in 1790. He is reported to have said to a friend, 'I believe we must adjourn this meeting to some other place.'

A conference is a gathering of important people who singly can do nothing but together decide that nothing can be done.
– FRED ALLEN

Meetings ... are rather like cocktail parties. You don't want to go, but you're cross not to be asked.
– JILLY COOPER

The Law of Triviality ... means that the time spent on any item of the agenda will be in inverse proportion to the sum involved.
– C. NORTHCOTE PARKINSON

Committees have become so important nowadays that subcommittees have to be appointed to do the work.
– LAURENCE J. PETER

The length of a meeting rises with the square of the number of people present.
– EILEEN SHANAHAN

My life's been a meeting ... one long meeting. Even on the few committees I don't yet belong to the agenda winks at me when I pass.
– GWYN THOMAS

* * *

Memory

see also Celebrity, Past

The desire to leave some kind of memory, more lasting than what Longfellow called 'footprints in the sands of time', is a deeply human one. Even those whose fame now seems unquestionable may have been concerned about it. Charles I's last word on the scaffold, spoken to Bishop Juxon, is said to have been 'Remember' (although there have been various interpretations of his precise meaning). Two centuries later, the dying Keats chose for his epitaph, 'Here lies one whose name was writ in water.' The lines of Laurence Binyon traditionally spoken at Remembrance Services conclude with the affirmation, 'We will remember them.' The beatnik writer Jack Kerouac had a particular view of the importance of being remembered: 'I hope it is true that a man can die and yet not only live in others but give them life, and not only life, but that great consciousness of life.'

Memories are not always pleasurable: in the phrase of Walter Savage Landor, they may engender 'a night of memories and sighs'. They may however come to contrast vividly with the present. Beryl Bainbridge has pointed out that 'The older one becomes the quicker the present fades into sepia and the past looms up in glorious technicolour.'

The ability to remember, or to forget, has practical implications. The seventeenth-century republican Algernon Sidney, executed for treason, wrote grimly that 'Liars ought to have good memories.' On the other hand, a poor memory can be a useful alibi. The French moralist La Rochefoucauld noted in 1678 that 'Everyone complains of his memory; nobody of his judgement.' In Robert Louis Stevenson's *Kidnapped*, Alan Breck reassured David Balfour, 'I've a grand memory for forgetting.'

God gave us memory so that we might have roses in
December.
– J. M. BARRIE

Everybody needs his memories. They keep the wolf of
insignificance from the door.
– SAUL BELLOW

One needs a good memory after telling lies.
– PIERRE CORNEILLE

The two offices of memory are collection and
distribution.
– SAMUEL JOHNSON

I have never tried to block out memories of the past, even
though some are painful ... Everything you live through
helps to make you the person you are now.
– SOPHIA LOREN

To expect a man to retain everything he has ever read is
like expecting him to carry about in his body everything
that he has ever eaten.
– ARTHUR SCHOPENHAUER

* * *

Men

see also Women

Kipling's poem *If*, with its concluding line 'You'll be a man, my son', set out one template for manliness: someone who can keep their head in any circumstance without being upset or disheartened. Tennyson, in *Idylls of the King*, wrote of 'The desire of fame, And love of truth, and all that makes a man'. A paragon on these lines might have had much in common with those who, according to George Orwell, followed 'a cult of cheeriness and manliness, beer and cricket, briar pipes and monogamy'. He would have understood the character sketched by Reginald Hill in one of his Dalziel and Pascoe stories: 'A man who was hard of head, blunt of speech, knew which side his bread was buttered on, and above all took no notice of women.' He would probably have conformed to the dictum of Mrs Gaskell's *Cranford*: 'A man ... is *so* in the way in the house', and might have fitted into the 'Men are from Mars and women are from Venus' mould of Erma Bombeck's exasperated question, 'What's wrong with you men? Would hair stop growing on your chest if you asked directions somewhere?'

Other female views of the male sex are more enthusiastic, perhaps responding to a type exemplified by Daisy Ashford's Mr Salteena. He confessed, 'I am parshial to ladies if they are nice. I suppose it is my nature.'

Women tell men things that men are not very likely to find out for themselves.
– ROBERTSON DAVIES

Men are clumsy, stupid creatures regarding little
things, but in their right place they are wonderful
animals.
– MILES FRANKLIN

Years ago, manhood was an opportunity for
achievement, and now it is a problem to be
overcome.
– GARRISON KEILLOR

A proper man, as one shall see on a summer's day.
– WILLIAM SHAKESPEARE

No nice men are good at getting taxis.
– KATHARINE WHITEHORN

Men play the game; women know the score.
– ROGER WODDIS

* * *

Middle Age

see also Age, Youth

Middle Age may be seen as an indeterminate stage between
age and youth. In Shakespeare's *Henry IV, Part 2*, Falstaff
asserted that the Chief Justice, while not being 'clean past'
his youth, did have 'some smack of age'. At the beginning

of the eighteenth century, Daniel Defoe gave a more positive picture of this mix: 'I've youth without its levity And age without decay.'

Certain ages are particularly associated with middle age, often in a decidedly negative way. At the beginning of the twentieth century, the Canadian-born physician William Osler gave a lecture in Baltimore entitled 'The comparative uselessness of men over forty years of age'. Commenting on this, the critic and journalist H. L. Mencken noted that 'This led to the misapprehension that Dr Osler proposed to retire, or even chloroform, all men at 40, and to the appearance of the verb *to oslerize*.'

Physical effects are often commented on. In *The Lady of the Lake*, Sir Walter Scott wrote of one of his characters that 'On his bold visage middle age Had slightly pressed its signet sage.' In the twentieth century, the American humorist Franklin P. Adams felt that it was possible to locate the 'dead centre' of middle age: 'It occurs when you are too old to rush up to the net, and too young to take up golf.' Or in a modern variant by Ian Pattison's Rab C. Nesbitt, 'Too young for the bowling green, too old for Ecstasy.'

After these views, it can be a relief to find even qualified approval for this time of life in one of Saki's short stories: 'The young have aspirations that never come to pass, the old have reminiscences of what never happened. It's only the middle-aged who are really conscious of their limitations.'

I am past thirty, and three parts iced over.
– MATTHEW ARNOLD

Forty-seven is nothing at all, nor is any age unless you're a cheese.
– BILLIE BURKE

The really frightening thing about middle age is the knowledge that you'll grow out of it.
– DORIS DAY

The years between fifty and seventy are the hardest. You are always being asked to do things, and you are not yet decrepit enough to turn them down.
– QUEEN ELIZABETH, THE QUEEN MOTHER

Middle age is when your age starts to show around the middle.
– BOB HOPE

Middle age is when you're faced with two temptations and you choose the one that will get you home at nine o'clock.
– RONALD REAGAN
(on his sixty-sixth birthday)

The old believe everything: the middle-aged suspect everything: the young know everything.
– OSCAR WILDE

* * *

Money

see also **Success**

According to the Bible, the love of money is the root of all evil. This teaching was sardonically emended by the nine-teenth-century writer Samuel Butler: 'It has been said that the love of money is the root of all evil. The want of money is so quite as truly.'

Whether or not money is loved, its supply has always been a matter of concern, both in affairs of state and private life. In classical Rome, Cicero saw unlimited money as 'the sinews of war', and the degree of limitation of available funds has evoked a variety of comment. At the beginning of the nineteenth cen-tury, it was said of John George Lambton, first Earl of Durham, that 'he considered £40,000 a year a moderate income – such a one as a man might *jog on* with'. (The diarist Thomas Creevey nicknamed him 'King Jog' in response to this.) At the other end of the social and economic scale, Dickens's Mr Micawber based his calculations on much narrower resources: 'Annual income twenty pounds, annual expenditure nineteen nine-teen and six, result happiness. Annual income twenty pounds, annual expenditure twenty pounds ought and six, result mis-ery.' In the twenty-first century, Bernie Ecclestone's daughter Tamara was reported as explaining carefully that there were indeed limits to their resources: 'Our jets don't have bath-rooms and I was driven to lessons in my mum's Audi.'

Proverbial wisdom is that 'Money cannot buy happiness', but it is not difficult to find proponents for the pursuit of wealth. The simple slogan 'To get rich is glorious' was adopted in China in the early 1980s, under the guidance of Deng Xiaoping.

A man who has a million dollars is as well off as if he were rich.
– JOHN JACOB ASTOR

There are rich people, and there are those who have money. They are not the same people.
– COCO CHANEL

My difficulty is trying to reconcile my gross habits with my net income.
– ERROL FLYNN

They who are of opinion that money will do everything may very well be suspected to do everything for money.
– LORD HALIFAX

All I ask is the chance to prove that money can't make me happy.
– SPIKE MILLIGAN

Always try to rub up against money, for if you rub up against money some of it may rub off on you.
– DAMON RUNYON

* * *

Mothers

see also Babies, Children, Families, Fathers, Parents

From the nursery poem of Ann and Jane Taylor ('Who ran to kiss me when I fell...? My Mother') to Kipling's ballad 'Mother o' Mine', nineteenth-century writings are full of praise of the maternal virtues of love and duty. 'What do girls do who haven't any mothers to help them through their troubles?' wondered Louisa Alcott's Jo March. A mother might set standards of behaviour (Anne Hunter's 'My mother bids me bind my hair' was often sung in drawing-rooms), but she loved her children unreservedly. This had its dangers, as demonstrated by the denouement of the 1874 stage adaptation of Mrs Henry Wood's novel *East Lynne*. The runaway wife, who has somewhat improbably returned to her former home in the disguise of a governess, is forced to witness unrecognized the deathbed of one of her own children. Her cry of 'Dead! and ....never called me mother' was clearly expected to touch the heartstrings of the audience of the day.

Oscar Wilde, rather than being touched, might have produced a variant of his comment on the death of Little Nell: that one would need a 'heart of stone' not to laugh.

Other and later writers have also taken a more objective view of motherhood, and its pains and penalties. After Jimmy Carter had been nominated by the Democratic Convention for a second presidential term, his mother 'Miss Lillian' said dryly, 'Sometimes when I look at my children I say to myself,

"Lillian, you should have stayed a virgin."' The journalist Barbara Ehrenreich has commented of motherhood that 'Nobody ever thought of putting it on a moral pedestal until some brash feminists pointed out, about a century ago, that the pay is lousy and the career ladder non-existent.'

On a more uplifting note, the African-American writer Zora Neale Hurston is on record with a wholehearted tribute to her mother's influence: 'Mama exhorted her children at every opportunity to "jump at de sun." We might not land on the sun, but at least we would get off the ground.'

To describe my mother would be to write about a hurricane in its perfect power.
– MAYA ANGELOU

A mother, who is really a mother, is never free.
– HONORÉ DE BALZAC

There is nothing more thrilling in this world, I think, than having a child that is yours and yet is mysteriously a stranger.
– AGATHA CHRISTIE

A mother's role is to deliver children – obstetrically once, and by car forever after.
– PETER DE VRIES

**When she'd had her first baby she realised with
astonishment that the perfect couple consisted of
mother and child and not, as she had always supposed, a
man and woman.**
– ALICE THOMAS ELLIS

**By and large, mothers and housewives are the only
workers who do not have regular time off. They are the
great vacationless class.**
– ANNE MORROW LINDBERGH

* * *

Music

'If music be the food of love, play on,' commanded Orsino in
Shakespeare's *Twelfth Night*. Orsino was speaking for music
lovers: the audience, but across the centuries we can also
hear the voices of 'the music makers': those whom Arthur
William O'Shaughnessy named 'the dreamers of dreams ...
World losers, and world forsakers'.

Sometimes a music maker finds their audience a trial.
The conductor Sir Thomas Beecham once said dryly that
'The English may not like music, but they absolutely love
the sound it makes.' This kind of qualified appreciation was
presumably exemplified by Bottom the Weaver in Shakespeare's *A Midsummer Night's Dream*, when he claimed, 'I have
a reasonable good ear in music. Let's have the tongs and the

bones.' The narrator in Mrs Gaskell's *Cranford*, describing an evening party at which music featured, noted that 'We were none of us musical, though Miss Jenkyns beat time, out of time, by way of appearing to be so.' Eric Morecambe in one sketch had a dignified defence of his performance: 'I am playing all the right notes, but not necessarily in the right order.'

Debussy said of one of Grieg's concertos that it resembled 'a pink bonbon filled with snow'. However, musicians can also show a generous appreciation of each other. When the musician and composer Thomas Tallis died in 1585, his fellow-musician William Byrd composed a madrigal of which the last line ran, 'Tallis is dead, and music dies.' But music, of course, continued to live: at the beginning of the nineteenth century, the composer Franz Schubert confided to his diary his admiration of 'Immortal Mozart'.

Music, the greatest good that mortals know.
– JOSEPH ADDISON

Where words fail, music speaks.
– HANS CHRISTIAN ANDERSEN

What passion cannot Music raise and quell?
– JOHN DRYDEN

Never compose anything unless the not composing of it becomes a positive nuisance.
– GUSTAV HOLST

Music is your own experience, your thoughts, your wisdom. If you don't live it, it won't come out of your horn.
– CHARLIE PARKER

The notes I handle no better than many pianists. But the pauses between the notes – that is where the art resides.
– ARTUR SCHNABEL

* * *

Nature

see also Gardens, Progress, Technology

Phrases such as 'greenhouse gases' and 'global warming', now a familiar part of the language, reflect concerns today about what we may be doing to our planet. Anxieties about a human tendency to spoliation, however, go back beyond our own time. Havelock Ellis wrote in 1923 that 'The sun, the moon and the stars would have disappeared long ago … had they happened to be within the reach of predatory human hands.'

The view of the natural world as something to be treasured is reflected in a line from the *Book of Common Prayer*: 'O all ye Green Things upon the Earth, bless ye the Lord.' It would have struck a chord with the scientist Marie Curie, who noted that 'All my life through, the new sights of Nature made me rejoice like a child.' And the practical importance of 'green things' has also been commented on: in the early nineteenth century, Pitt the Elder was quoted as calling London's parks 'the lungs of London'.

There are also some robust voices which speak up for the durability of nature. The Roman poet Horace thought that 'You may drive out Nature with a pitchfork, but she always comes hurrying back.' Impatience resonates, perhaps predictably, in the assertion of Jeremy Clarkson: 'There will be no leaf, tree, cloud, lawn, peat bog or environmental precious place that I won't drive over.' But against these views, we have a dry comment from the mid nineteenth century in a letter from the naturalist Henry David Thoreau: 'What is the use of a house if you haven't got a tolerable planet to put it on?'

After one look at this planet any visitor from outer space would say 'I want to see the manager.'
– WILLIAM S. BURROUGHS

There is nothing so strong as growing. Nothing can drown the force that splits rocks and pavements and spreads over the fields.
– EMILY CARR

It is a law of the natural universe that no being can exist on its own resources. Everyone, everything, is hopelessly indebted to everyone and everything else.
– C. S. LEWIS

The middle classes think they have gone green because they have bought organic cotton pyjamas and use handmade soap with bits of leaf in it.
– GEORGE MONBIOT

Let us a little permit Nature to take her own ways; she better understands her own affairs than we.
– MICHEL DE MONTAIGNE

People from a planet without flowers would think we must be mad with joy the whole time to have such things about us.
– IRIS MURDOCH

The smallest sprout shows there is really no death.
– WALT WHITMAN

* * *

Opportunity

see also Business, Hope, Luck

From 'Strike while the iron is hot' to 'Opportunity seldom knocks twice', proverbial advice on opportunity is likely to advise taking what is offered while it is available. In Shakespeare's *Julius Caesar*, Brutus told Cassius that 'There is a tide in the affairs of men Which, taken at the flood, leads on to fortune', and warned that omitting to take the tide would ensure that 'the voyage of their life' would be 'bound in shallows and in miseries'. The subsequent history of Brutus and Cassius does not in fact suggest that in this case eagerness to catch the tide was helpful. Their decision might be characterized in Juliet's words as 'too rash, too unadvised, too sudden'. But while seizing an opportunity must always carry some risk (Byron reworked Shakespeare's lines to read 'There is a tide in the affairs of women, Which, taken at the flood, leads – God knows where'), the advice against missing a chance is overwhelming.

Apart from the question of whether an opportunity should be taken, there is also advice on the tactics to be used. Montaigne recommended that 'One should always have one's boots on and be ready to go.' The Canadian bacteriologist Oswald Theodore Avery is said to have advised, 'Whenever you fall, pick up something.' Stephen Potter saw an advantage in disadvantaging someone else. In his view, the way to be one up was to 'make the other man feel that something has gone wrong, however slightly'. During a moment of crisis, Homer Simpson had his eye on the essentials, telling himself, 'Keep looking shocked and move slowly towards the cakes.'

On the keyboard of life, always keep one finger on the escape key.
– SCOTT ADAMS
(from the world of Dilbert)

A wise man will make more opportunities than he finds.
– FRANCIS BACON

There is far more opportunity than there is ability.
– THOMAS EDISON

Problems are only opportunities in work clothes.
– HENRY J. KAISER

Any human being anywhere will blossom into a hundred unexpected talents and capacities simply by being given the opportunity to use them.
– DORIS LESSING

There is no security on this earth, only opportunity.
– DOUGLAS MACARTHUR

The follies which a man most regrets in his life are those which he didn't commit when he had the opportunity.
– HELEN ROWLAND

* * *

Parents

see also Babies, Children, Families, Fathers, Mothers

According to a modern saying variously attributed to the nineteenth-century writer Samuel Butler and an unidentified English headmaster, 'Parents are the last people on earth who ought to have children.' George Bernard Shaw reflected that 'Parentage is a very important profession; but no test of

fitness for it is ever imposed in the interests of the children.'
Philip Larkin's 'This be the Verse' famously, and succinctly,
invoked the negative impact that parents can have on their
offspring, filling their children with their own faults and
adding some extra: 'They may not mean to, but they do.' In
his novel *A Buyer's Market*, Anthony Powell reflected that 'Parents – especially step-parents – are sometimes a bit of a disappointment to their children. They don't fulfil the promise of
their early years.'

Against this, it must also be admitted that children can
be a critical audience for their begetters. In the eighteenth
century, Laurence Sterne's Tristram Shandy said dispassion-
ately, 'I wish either my father or my mother, or indeed both
of them, had minded what they were about when they begot
me.' And the historian Edward Gibbon wrote alarmingly
in his *Memoirs*, 'The tears of a son are seldom lasting ... Few
perhaps are the children who, after the expiration of some
months or years, would sincerely rejoice in the resurrection
of their parents.' It is a relief after this bleak picture to turn
to the more optimistic view of the Canadian writer Margaret
Laurence: 'If, as you grow older, you feel you are also growing
stupider, do not worry. This is normal, and usually occurs
around the time when your children, now grown, are discovering the opposite – they now see that you aren't nearly as
stupid as they had believed when they were young teenagers.
Take heart from that.'

The joys of parents are secret, and so are their griefs and fears.
– FRANCIS BACON

When my kids become wild and unruly, I use a nice, safe playpen. When they're finished, I climb out.
– ERMA BOMBECK

It is not a bad thing that children should occasionally, and politely, put parents in their place.
– COLETTE

The thing that impresses me about America is the way parents obey their children.
– EDWARD VIII

What a child doesn't receive he can seldom later give.
– P. D. JAMES

If you bungle raising your children, nothing else much matters in life.
– JACQUELINE KENNEDY ONASSIS

Parents learn a lot from their children about coping with life.
– MURIEL SPARK

* * *

The Past

see also **Future, Memory, Present, Time**

L. P. Hartley wrote that 'The past is a foreign country; they do things differently there', and for many that sense of separation from the past has been a matter of deep regret. Its memory may illuminate lost ideals. 'Never glad confident morning again!' wrote Robert Browning, in an expression that has entered the language, when Wordsworth was seen to have betrayed the radical principles of his youth by accepting the position of poet laureate. A. E. Housman in *A Shropshire Lad* coined elegiac phrases like 'those blue remembered hills' and 'the land of lost content' in his nostalgic evocation of the 'happy highways' where he 'went And cannot come again'.

The French writer Colette, on the other hand, while admitting this view of a lost Elysium, thought that it posed a conundrum: 'But the past, the beautiful past striped with sunshine, grey with mist, childish, blooming with hidden joy, bruised with sweet sorrow ... Ah! If only I could resurrect one hour of that time, one alone – but which one?' And the Anglican clergyman Dean Inge was cautionary about cherished memories: 'The things which we know about the past may be divided into those which probably never happened and those which do not much matter.' For many, however, the novelist Penelope Fitzgerald probably touched a chord when she drew her wishes for the New Year from a vision of the past: 'Conductors should be back on the buses, packets of salt back in the crisps, clockwork back in the clocks and levers back in pens.'

A safe but sometimes chilly way of recalling the past is to force open a crammed drawer. If you are searching for anything in particular you don't find it, but something falls out at the back that is often more interesting.
– J. M. Barrie

If past history is all there was to the game, the richest people would be librarians.
– Warren Buffett
(on the art of investing)

The past is not a package one can lay away.
– Emily Dickinson

If the past cannot teach the present and the father cannot teach the son, then history need not have bothered to go on, and the world has wasted a great deal of time.
– Russell Hoban

You have to know the past to understand the present.
– Carl Sagan

Those who cannot remember the past are condemned to repeat it.
– George Santayana

*   *   *

Patience

see also Hope, Opportunity

The proverbial advice that 'Patience is a virtue' has been part of the language since the Middle Ages, perhaps reinforced by the thought that 'Everything comes to him who waits.' In the seventeenth century, Jean de la Fontaine thought that 'Patience and time do more than force and rage.'

There are also however a number of voices which, over the centuries, have seen a certain danger in being too ready to wait for what might be given. In Shakespeare's *Twelfth Night*, Viola's image of 'Patience on a monument, smiling at grief' is hardly an encouraging one. The seventeenth-century playwright Philip Massinger referred to 'Patience, the beggar's virtue'.

Edmund Burke warned that 'There is a limit at which forbearance ceases to be a virtue', a view neatly illustrated by Anthony Trollope: 'It is because we put up with bad things that hotel-keepers continue to give them to us.' By the beginning of the twentieth century Ambrose Bierce's *Cynic's Word Book* contained the entry, 'Patience. A minor form of despair, disguised as a virtue.' The definition is in accord with a wry comment by the nineteenth-century novelist Samuel Butler. He reworked Goldsmith's 'Man wants but little here below, nor wants that little long' to '"Man wants but little here below" but likes that little good – and not too long in coming.'

Beware the fury of a patient man.
– JOHN DRYDEN

Patience, that blending of moral courage with physical
timidity.
– THOMAS HARDY

To know how to wait is the great secret of success.
– JOSEPH DE MAISTRE

Impatience is the mark of independence, not of bondage.
– MARIANNE MOORE

If he had made any advances in those subjects, it was
owing more to patient attention than to any other talent.
– ISAAC NEWTON
(complimented on his work in mathematics and natural
 philosophy)

I am extraordinarily patient, provided I get my own way
in the end.
– MARGARET THATCHER

The old maxim that 'Everything comes to him who waits'
is all very well provided he knows what he is waiting for.
– WOODROW WILSON

*　*　*

Politics

'Man is by nature a political animal,' said Aristotle, and since his time many of those political animals have commented on the political world. In the eighteenth century, Samuel Johnson thought that politics had become 'nothing more than a means of rising in the world'. Dr Johnson might not have been surprised, looking down the years, to hear Alan Clark's view that 'There are no true friends in politics. We are all sharks circling and waiting for traces of blood to appear in the water.' (Ruthless competition, of course, is only part of the picture. Matthew Parris, commenting on what he saw as a particularly sycophantic question put to Tony Blair as Prime Minister by a Labour backbencher, wrote, 'To call it toadying would be to invite a group libel action from toads.')

Bismarck, the Iron Chancellor, thought that 'Politics is the art of the possible.' In some ways, that is a view echoed by Disraeli's 'Finality is not the language of politics.' However, there may be problems from the outset: Samuel Taylor Coleridge warned that 'In politics, what begins in fear usually ends in folly.' In the twentieth century, Vera Brittain thought that 'Politics are usually the executive expression of human immaturity.'

Most of these comments come from those who were either part of the political world, or at least familiar with it. However, many of those who vote have to make a choice from little or no personal knowledge of a candidate. The American

humorist 'Kin' Hubbard highlighted the difficulty by point-
ing out that while everyone would like to vote for the 'best
man, he's never a candidate'. It can be tempting to adopt a
cynical approach, perhaps agreeing with another American
humorist, Will Rogers, that 'The more you read ... about this
Politics thing, you got to admit that each party is worse than
the other.' But against this can be set a simple statement from
a statesman who has come near to commanding universal
admiration. Nelson Mandela wrote in 1961, 'The struggle is
my life.'

**Being an MP is the sort of job all working-class parents
want for their children – clean, indoors and no heavy
lifting.**
– DIANE ABBOTT

**The only safe pleasure for a parliamentarian is a bag of
boiled sweets.**
– JULIAN CRITCHLEY

Politics is the art of human happiness.
– H. A. L. FISHER

**There are times in politics when you must be on the
right side and lose.**
– JOHN KENNETH GALBRAITH

If men were angels, no government would be necessary.
– JAMES MADISON

Every politician should have three hats handy at all times: one for throwing into the ring, one for talking through, and a third for pulling rabbits out of if elected.
– CARL SANDBURG

* * *

The Present

see also Future, Past, Time

There are two approaches to the present. One is to believe, often with great regret, that it is less good than the receding, and somehow golden, past. In the eighteenth century, Edmund Burke wrote, 'To complain of the age we live in, to murmur at the present possessors of power, to lament the past ... are the common dispositions of the greatest part of mankind.' Or, as Benjamin Franklin said succinctly, 'The golden age never was the present age.' Two centuries later, the American comedian Art Buchwald, giving a commencement address at Vassar in 1975, expressed his essential scepticism about this approach. Having said that he himself did not think that 'yesterday was better than today', he continued, 'I would advise you not to wait ten years before admitting today was great. If you're hung up on nostalgia, pretend today is yesterday and just go out and have one hell of a time.'

The other way of dealing with the present is to take the attitude recommended by the seventeenth-century poet

Robert Herrick, 'Gather ye rosebuds while ye may.' In this view, the present is precious because it is fleeting, and we fail to take advantage of it at our peril. As Ralph Waldo Emerson wrote in his journal, 'With the Past, as past, I have nothing to do; nor with the Future as future. I live now.'

The present offers exciting possibilities, but it is not necessarily the safe option. Joan Collins is on record with a very upbeat assessment: 'Yesterday is history, tomorrow's a mystery, but today is a gift ... That's why it's called the present.' Against this, however, we have an implicit warning from Arthur Miller in the 1960s: 'The word now is like a bomb through the window, and it ticks.'

Tomorrow do thy worst, for I have lived today.
– JOHN DRYDEN

Children enjoy the present because they have neither a past nor a future.
– JEAN DE LA BRUYÈRE

The living moment is everything.
– D. H. LAWRENCE

That virgin, vital, beautiful day: today.
– STÉPHANE MALLARMÉ

You must live in the present, launch yourself on every wave, find your eternity in each moment.
– HENRY DAVID THOREAU

The present is the ever-moving shadow that divides yesterday from tomorrow. In that lies hope.
– FRANK LLOYD WRIGHT

* * *

Progress

see also Change, Future, Technology

The nineteenth-century philosopher and writer Herbert Spencer saw progress as an unstoppable force, writing that 'Progress, therefore, is not an accident, but a necessity ... it is a part of nature.' However, while most people would probably agree with the general sentiment, there are a number of caveats as to the precise process. C. S. Lewis went into some detail about this: 'We all want progress. But progress means getting nearer to the place where you want to be ... If you are on the wrong road, progress means doing an about-turn and walking back to the right road; and in that case the man who turns back soonest is the most progressive man.' The philosopher George Santayana seems to have had a similar image in mind when he wrote, 'The cry was for freedom and indeterminate progress: *Vorwärts! Avanti!* Onwards! Full speed ahead!, without asking whether directly before you was not a bottomless pit.'

There are different views as to what might stimulate progress. Albert Einstein saw the key as being imagination: 'Imagination is more important than knowledge. For knowledge is limited, whereas imagination embraces the entire world, stimulating progress.' The novelist Samuel Butler, however, had a more cynical view: 'All progress is based upon a universal innate desire on the part of every organism to live beyond its income.'

We have stopped believing in progress. What progress that is!
– JORGE LUIS BORGES

All that is human must retrograde if it does not advance.
– EDWARD GIBBON

The world is moving so fast these days that the man who says it can't be done is generally interrupted by someone doing it.
– ELBERT HUBBARD

The chief obstacle to the progress of the human race is the human race.
– DON MARQUIS

Progress might have been all right once, but it's gone on too long.
– OGDEN NASH

**The reasonable man adapts himself to the world: the
unreasonable one persists in trying to adapt the world
to himself. Therefore all progress depends on the
unreasonable man.**
– GEORGE BERNARD SHAW

* * *

Publishing

see also Reading, Writing

'Go, litel bok,' wrote Geoffrey Chaucer, launching *Troilus
and Criseyde* upon the reading world. 'Publishing' in his day
depended on handwritten manuscripts; it was not until the
fifteenth century that the world was revolutionized by the
invention of printing: the development which Francis Bacon
considered to be one of three things (the other two were gun-
powder and the compass) which had 'changed the whole face
and state of things throughout the world'. In the nineteenth
century, Thomas Carlyle developed this picture: 'He who
first shortened the labour of copyists by device of movable
types was disbanding hired armies, and cashiering most
kings and senates, and creating a whole democratic world:
he had invented the art of printing.'

Bacon and Carlyle provide publishing with an impressive pedigree, but a number of subsequent quotations from
the field are less dignified. The courtesan Harriette Wilson
attempted to blackmail the Duke of Wellington by threatening to include a discreditable account of him in her memoirs,

196

only to receive the firm rejection, 'Publish and be damned!' It was a response which lodged itself in the language. In the twentieth century it was to be reworked by Richard Ingrams, who as Editor of *Private Eye* declared, 'My own motto is publish and be sued.'

Posterity – what you write for after being turned down by publishers.
– GEORGE ADE

If I had been someone not very clever, I would have done an easier job like publishing.
– A. J. AYER

Now Barabbas was a publisher.
– THOMAS CAMPBELL

As repressed sadists are supposed to become policemen or butchers so those with an irrational fear of life become publishers.
– CYRIL CONNOLLY

Publishers are demons, there's no doubt about it.
– WILLIAM JAMES

I did toy with the idea of doing a cook-book ... I think a lot of people who hate literature but love fried eggs would buy it if the price was right.
– GROUCHO MARX

* * *

Punctuality

see also Time

'Procrastination is the thief of time,' wrote the eighteenth-century poet and clergyman Edward Young. The saying, which has become proverbial, was reworked a century later by Oscar Wilde. In *The Picture of Dorian Gray*, Dorian is kept waiting by his hedonistic friend Lord Henry: 'He was always late on principle, his principle being that punctuality is the thief of time.' Other personal protests against punctuality can be found. Saville in Hannah Cowley's *The Belle's Stratagem*, told that he has missed someone by five minutes, exclaims, 'Five minutes! Zounds! I have been five minutes too late all my lifetime.' One of Robert Burns's poems was based on a traditional song beginning, 'Up in the morning's no for me, Up in the morning early.'

Lord Henry (a disastrous influence on Dorian) was a successful figure in London society, but would not have done well at French courts of earlier years. The proverbial 'Punctuality is the politeness of kings' is attributed to Louis XVIII. An earlier and more imperious king would have been less tolerant: Louis XIV is said to have commented unforgivingly on one occasion, 'I almost had to wait.'

For many, punctuality has been linked to order and good management. The eighteenth-century clergyman Richard Cecil recorded, 'Method, as Mrs More says, is the very hinge of business; and there is no method without punctuality.'

The chef Anthelme Brillat-Savarin thought that 'Of all the qualities, indispensable in a cook, punctuality is the foremost.' (He warned that if people who are ready to eat are kept waiting, they will give way to 'yawning, pangs and hunger'.) In the twentieth century, Winston Churchill said that 'Unpunctuality is a vile habit, and all my life I have tried to break myself of it.' However, the person who succeeds in being habitually punctual should probably be aware that this will not engender universal admiration. Evelyn Waugh's view in the 1960s was that 'Punctuality is the virtue of the bored.'

Never the time and the place,
And the loved one all together.
– ROBERT BROWNING

Punctuality is one of the cardinal business virtues.
Always insist on it in your subordinates.
– DON MARQUIS

I've been on a calendar, but never on time.
– MARILYN MONROE

I have always been a quarter of an hour before my time,
and it has made a man of me.
– LORD NELSON

Three o'clock is always too late or too early for anything you want to do.
– JEAN-PAUL SARTRE

Better three hours too soon, than a minute too late.
– WILLIAM SHAKESPEARE

* * *

Quotation

see also Language, Speechmaking, Writing

Ralph Waldo Emerson saw quotation as a natural tendency: 'By necessity, by proclivity – and by delight, we all quote.' There has, however, been no shortage of advice as to how, and what, we should quote. The seventeenth-century lawyer and scholar John Selden advised, 'In quoting of books, quote such authors as are usually read; others you may read for your own satisfaction, but not name them.' The eighteenth-century classical scholar Richard Bentley took this rather further, not to say to extremes. According to an anecdote, he once found his son reading a novel, and reproved him for thus wasting his time: 'Why read a book you cannot quote?' (Bentley was, of course, talking of quotation from a source which the quoter has read and knows well. He would have been shocked by a comment made by Kenneth Williams: 'The nicest thing about quotes is that they give us a nodding acquaintance with the originator which is often socially impressive.')

Evelyn Waugh once wrote that 'Quotation is a national vice.' The comment could be linked with a sentence from a review written by George Orwell about a book by the poet Edmund Blunden. Feeling that it was in some places rather over-written, he suggested a reason: 'Mr Blunden is no more able to resist a quotation than some people are to resist a drink.' The same idea of quotation as a personal indulgence appears in one of Amanda Cross's mystery stories. Her series detective, Kate Fansler, once confessed, 'Quoting, like smoking, is a dirty habit to which I am devoted.'

It is a good thing for an uneducated man to read books of quotations.
– WINSTON CHURCHILL

Classical quotation is the *parole* of the literary man.
– SAMUEL JOHNSON

Everything I've ever said will be credited to Dorothy Parker.
– GEORGE S. KAUFMAN

To be amused at what you read – that is the great spring of happy quotation.
– C. E. MONTAGUE

I quote others only in order the better to express myself.
– MICHEL DE MONTAIGNE

Misquotations are the only quotations that are never misquoted.
– HESKETH PEARSON

I often quote myself. It adds spice to my conversation.
– GEORGE BERNARD SHAW

* * *

Reading

see also Publishing, Writing

'Reading', said Francis Bacon, 'maketh a full man.' In this view, reading offers intellectual enrichment, but other comments also lay stress on the pleasure of the activity. 'I have always imagined that Paradise will be a kind of library,' wrote Jorge Luis Borges. The critic Logan Pearsall Smith went further, asserting, 'People say that life is the thing, but I prefer reading.' Perhaps, however, the distinction between reading and life is a false one: in the film *Shadowlands*, C. S. Lewis hears and then quotes approvingly the view that 'We read to know we're not alone.'

John Thorpe, in Jane Austen's *Northanger Abbey*, took a very different approach. When Catherine Morland asked if he had read *Udolpho*, he replied sweepingly, 'I never read novels; I have something else to do.' (He justified this literary opinion by adding that novels were 'all so full of nonsense and stuff'.) He would probably have understood Victoria Beckham, who was quoted in a 2005 interview as saying, 'I haven't read a book in my life. I haven't the time.'

These opposing views both consider reading as a source of pleasure, but of course there are other reasons to pick up a book. The action itself may stimulate creativity: as George Crabbe wrote, 'Who often reads, will sometimes wish to write.' It may, however, have other effects. The writer Arthur Helps said, 'Reading is sometimes an ingenious device for avoiding thought.' More dramatically, Jack Kerouac reflected on the effect that reading his *On the Road* had on many in the 1960s: '*On the Road* sold a trillion Levis and a million espresso machines, and also sent countless kids on the road.'

The book is the world's most patient medium.
– NORTHROP FRYE

The art of reading is to skip judiciously.
– P. G. HAMERTON

To learn to read is to light a fire. Every syllable spelled out is a spark.
– VICTOR HUGO

There are two motives for reading a book: one, that you enjoy it, the other that you can boast about it.
– BERTRAND RUSSELL

**The more that you read, the more things you will know.
The more that you learn, the more places you'll go.**
– DR SEUSS

**If one cannot enjoy reading a book over and over again,
there is no use reading it at all.**
– OSCAR WILDE

* * *

Relationships

see also Families, Friendship, Love

Relationships are often thought of only in terms of romantic love, and not always positively. In one of Kipling's stories, Mrs Mallowe tells her friend Mrs Hauksbee, 'My experience of men is that when they begin to quote poetry they are going to flit. Like swans singing before they die, you know.' The actress Katharine Hepburn once said, 'Sometimes I wonder if men and women really suit each other. Perhaps they should live next door and just visit now and then.' A more extreme position has been set out by Ruby Wax: 'This "relationship" business is one big waste of time. It is just Mother Nature urging you to breed, breed, breed. Learn from nature. Learn from our friend the spider. Just mate once and then kill him.'

Buffy the Vampire-Slayer's friend Willow, on the other hand, showed remarkable tolerance, even on discovering that her boyfriend was a werewolf. She reassured him: 'I like you. You're nice and you're funny and you don't smoke and okay, werewolf, but that's not all the time. I mean, three days out of the month I'm not much fun to be around either.'

Not all important relationships, however, are sexual. The nineteenth-century novelist Dinah Craik illuminates another aspect: 'Oh, the comfort – the inexpressible comfort of feeling safe with a person – having neither to weigh thoughts nor measure words, but pouring them all right out, just as they are, chaff and grain together.' Or, as Emily Dickinson wrote to a friend, 'I felt it shelter to speak to you.'

Thou art to me a delicious torment.
– RALPH WALDO EMERSON

Someone to tell it to is one of the fundamental needs of human beings.
– MILES FRANKLIN

People change and forget to tell each other.
– LILLIAN HELLMAN

Having someone wonder where you are when you don't come home at night is a very old human need.
– MARGARET MEAD

He's so lucky to be going out with me.
– KATE MIDDLETON
(to a friend who had said that she was 'so lucky to be going
out with Prince William')

**Man is a knot, a web, a mesh into which relationships are
tied.**
– ANTOINE DE SAINT-EXUPÉRY

* * *

Reputation

see also **Celebrity, Memory**

'My reputation, Iago, my reputation!' lamented the torment-
ed Othello, grieving for what he called 'the immortal part
of myself'. Since Shakespeare's time, there have been many
comments on the importance, and susceptibility to damage,
of the beliefs and opinions generally held about a person.
Reputation may or may not be associated with worldly success: Mark Twain's Yankee at the court of King Arthur noted
of the practice of seeking the Holy Grail ('holy grailing') that
'There was worlds of reputation in it, but no money.'

In one important area, a particular limitation was registered. Fanny Burney wrote at the end of the eighteenth century, 'Nothing is so delicate as the reputation of a woman; it
is at once the most beautiful and most brittle of all human
things.' By this stage, to 'lose your reputation' had a rather

different meaning from that given it by Shakespeare's suffering Moor of Venice. And reputations could be destroyed as well as lost; Swift's 'Journal of a Modern Lady' refers to those who are able to 'Convey a libel in a frown, And wink a reputation down.' Richard Brinsley Sheridan, considering a historical play, asked anxiously, 'No scandal about Queen Elizabeth, I hope?'

Once a reputation (male or female) had been lost, life could be difficult. George Eliot in her 1866 novel *Felix Holt* referred largely to '"Abroad", that large home of ruined reputations'. On the other hand, it is possible to overrate the individual effect of damage done. Mae West, describing the plot of her 1933 film *I'm No Angel*, explained, 'It's all about a girl who lost her reputation but never missed it.' Alan Clark, asked whether he had any embarrassing skeletons in the cupboard, responded insouciantly, 'Dear boy, I can hardly close the door.' And Warren Buffett has suggested that failure in a group may in difficult circumstances be the way to go: 'Lemmings may have a rotten image, but no individual lemming has yet received a bad press.'

Repetition makes reputation, and reputation makes customers.
– ELIZABETH ARDEN

The invisible thing called a good name is made up of the breath of numbers that speak well of you.
– LORD HALIFAX

Character is like a tree and reputation like its shadow. The shadow is what we think of it; the tree is the real thing.
– ABRAHAM LINCOLN

Reputation is in itself only a farthing-candle, of wavering and uncertain flame, and easily blown out, but it is the light by which the world looks for and finds merit.
– JAMES RUSSELL LOWELL

Until you've lost your reputation you never realize what a burden it was or what freedom really is.
– MARGARET MITCHELL

My reputation grows with every failure.
– GEORGE BERNARD SHAW

* * *

Retirement

see also Careers, Leisure, Work

In the eighteenth century James Thomson could write lyrically of 'Retirement, rural quiet, friendship, books', but even in that more leisured time his near-contemporary William Cowper was to point out that 'Absence of occupation is not rest.' Ernest Hemingway has been quoted as saying that 'Retirement is the ugliest word in the language.' The financier Bernard Baruch, when asked his opinion, responded, 'I do not believe in discarding human beings.' However, whatever our perspective, in the twenty-first century it is inevitable that we will at some point need to grapple with the concept, and indeed the actuality, of retirement.

An early model was set by the third President of the United States, Thomas Jefferson. He wrote to a friend in 1805, 'General Washington set the example of voluntary retirement after eight years. I shall follow it.' The precedent set by Washington and Jefferson was eventually enshrined in law, so that when in 2007 George W. Bush made public the retirement of his long-time adviser Karl Rove, he could add without causing surprise, 'I'll be on the road behind you in a little bit.'

It can be difficult for someone to detach themselves from a particular world. The film mogul Jack Warner commented that 'You're nothing if you don't have a studio. Now I'm just another millionaire.' Steve Redgrave, having won his fourth Olympic gold medal at Atlanta in 1996, announced his retirement with the words, 'If you see me getting in a boat again you have my full permission to shoot me.' He used strikingly similar words – 'I hereby give permission to anyone who catches me in a boat again to shoot me' – after winning Olympic gold for the fifth time, this time at Sydney, in 2000.

Perhaps the key to successful retirement is seeing it as a move to something new that you want to do. Tolkien's Bilbo Baggins, for one, had definite plans: 'I want to see mountains again, Gandalf – *mountains*. And then find somewhere where I can rest ... I might find somewhere where I can finish my book.'

I want to get out with my greatness intact.
– Muhammad Ali

Retirement ... may be looked upon either as a prolonged holiday or as a rejection, a being thrown on to the scrap-heap.
– Simone de Beauvoir

The question isn't at what age I want to retire, it's at what income.
– George Foreman

When a man retires, he has to retire to something.
– Harry Emerson Fosdick

Sooner or later, I'm going to die, but I'm not going to retire.
– Margaret Mead

I have made noise enough in the world already, perhaps too much, and am now getting old, and want retirement.
– Napoleon

People always say to me, 'When are you going to retire?' Retire and do what? Tell my mailman jokes?
– Joan Rivers

* * *

Science

see also Knowledge, Technology

In any collection of quotations about science, a range of voices speak of the difficulties and delights of scientific discovery. Michael Faraday illuminated the necessarily hopeful nature of research when he wrote in a letter of 1831, 'I am busy just now again on Electro-Magnetism and think I have got hold of a good thing but can't say; it may be a weed instead of a fish that after all my labour I may at last pull up.' The image suggests clearly the potential disappointment of the researcher: what Thomas Henry Huxley called 'The great tragedy of Science – the slaying of a beautiful hypothesis by an ugly fact'. Delight, on the other hand, was what informed Francis Crick's summary of the discovery of the structure of DNA in 1953: 'We have discovered the secret of life!'

Faraday's caution would have been approved by James Jeans, who warned against the dangers of making predictions: 'Science should leave off making pronouncements: the river of knowledge has too often turned back on itself.' Nearly forty years later, Arthur C. Clarke took a similar, if more detailed, line: 'When a distinguished but elderly scientist states that something is possible, he is almost certainly right. When he states that something is impossible, he is very probably wrong.'

That is the essence of science: ask an impertinent question, and you are on your way to the pertinent answer.

– JACOB BRONOWSKI

A theory can be proved by experiment; but no path leads from experiment to the birth of a theory.
– ALBERT EINSTEIN

Scientific discovery is a private event, and the delight that accompanies it, or the despair of finding it illusory does not travel.
– PETER MEDAWAR

If I have seen further it is by standing on the shoulders of giants.
– ISAAC NEWTON

A new scientific truth does not triumph by convincing its opponents and making them see the light, but rather because its opponents eventually die, and a new generation grows up that is familiar with it.
– MAX PLANCK

* * *

Shopping

see also Leisure, Money

The consumerist 1980s saw the coinage of such expressions as 'shop till you drop' and 'retail therapy', but the perception of shopping as an enjoyable, and even restorative, indulgence is not merely a modern phenomenon. In Susan

Ferrier's 1824 novel *The Inheritance*, we read, 'Still Gertrude did not feel happy; but the usual panacea was applied.' The 'usual panacea' is further explained as 'squandering money in dissipating thought'. Or, as Arthur Miller was to put it in the twentieth century, 'Today you're unhappy? Can't figure it out? What is the salvation? Go shopping.' Although it may not always be straightforward. In 2003, accounts of the first episode of a reality show featuring the American heiress Paris Hilton included her bewilderment at a reference to the store Wal-Mart. 'Is it, like, where they sell wall stuff?'

Shopping was presumably even more pleasurable for someone already in good spirits. The 1832 diary of the traveller Prince von Pückler-Muskau recorded a recognizable account of a leisured tourist. He wrote, 'In the morning I see sights, saunter from one museum to another, or go "shopping". (This word signifies to go from shop to shop buying trifles, such as luxury is always inventing in Paris and London.)' Such shopping might, have course, have been very expensive. Mary Russell Mitford's 1829 *Our Village* gave a picture of someone whose judgement might well be overwhelmed. In this context, the narrator has prepared in advance a shopping list with predicted prices, but finds that her budgeting has not been well founded. She was 'A little astonished, at first, to find everything so much dearer than I had set it down, yet soon reconciled to this misfortune by the magical influence which shopping possesses over a woman's fancy.' It was presumably a variant of this magical influence which was felt by Cher Horowitz in the 1990s film *Clueless*. On her way to the shopping mall, she explained, 'I had to find sanctuary in a place where I could gather my thoughts and regain my strength.'

We used to build civilizations. Now we build shopping malls.
– BILL BRYSON

Fine meals require ingenious organization and experience which is a pleasure to acquire. A highly developed shopping sense is important.
– ELIZABETH DAVID

Americans are fascinated by their own love of shopping. This does not make them unique. It's just that they have more to buy than most other people on the planet.
– SIMON HOGGART

People will buy anything that's one to a customer.
– SINCLAIR LEWIS

I'm going to spend, spend, spend.
– VIVIAN NICHOLSON
(asked what she would do with the £152,000 she won on the pools in 1961)

If you think the United States has stood still, who built the largest shopping centre in the world?
– RICHARD NIXON

214

I like to walk down Bond Street, thinking of all the things I don't desire.
– LOGAN PEARSALL SMITH

Getting and spending, we lay waste our powers.
– WILLIAM WORDSWORTH

* * *

Single Life

see also Marriage, Relationships

Francis Bacon in the sixteenth century had suggested that for men at least the single life might be an option: 'He was reputed one of the wise men that made answer to the question when a man should marry? "A young man not yet, and elder man not at all."' Two centuries later, that approach would have been condemned by ladies, like Jane Austen's Mrs Bennett, who were concerned to find husbands for their daughters. Their view is expressed in the famous opening words of *Pride and Prejudice*: 'It is a truth universally acknowledged, that a single man in possession of a good fortune, must be in want of a wife.'

In Shakespeare's *A Midsummer Night's Dream*, Hermia was warned that if she would not marry the man of her father's choice she must live out her life 'in single blessedness': it is clear from the context that this was expected to be an unwelcome prospect. In the twentieth century, Nancy Mitford suggested that even the hope of marriage might be important: '"Always be civil to the girls, you never know who they may marry"' is an aphorism which has saved many an English spinster from being treated like an Indian widow.' Bridget Jones, the fictional diarist created by Helen Fielding, was perennially uncomfortable with her single state, and had fantasies about 'being trendy Smug Married instead of sheepish Singleton'. She might with advantage have listened to the dry comment of American writer Edna Ferber, 'Being an old maid is like death by drowning, a really delightful sensation after you cease to struggle.'

I would be married, but I'd have no wife,
I would be married to a single life.
– RICHARD CRASHAW

A man … is so in the way in a house!
– ELIZABETH GASKELL

I was born to be a spinster, and by God, I'm going to spin.
– WINIFRED HOLTBY

A woman is only a woman, but a good cigar is a smoke!
– RUDYARD KIPLING

Never trust a husband too far or a bachelor too near.
– HELEN ROWLAND

I never found the companion that was so companionable as solitude.
– Henry David Thoreau

* * *

Speechmaking

see also Language

Speechmaking is likely to require effort on the part of the speaker – effort which the person who has expended will not want to see wasted. In Shakespeare's *Twelfth Night*, when Viola disguised as the page Cesario comes to pay addresses to Olivia on Orsino's behalf, she is indignant at the idea that she should not deliver her prepared words: 'I would be loath to cast away my speech; for, besides that it is excellently well-penned, I have taken great pains to con it.' A similar determination can be traced in the words of Disraeli, concluding his maiden speech in the Commons in 1837. Feeling that he had not commanded his audience, he told them defiantly, 'Though I sit down now, the time will come when you will hear me.'

Not everyone is suited to public speaking. In Thomas Love Peacock's 1831 comic novel *Crotchet Castle*, Mr Skionair suggested that he could use his talents to dispel a crowd. 'Let me address them. I never failed to convince an audience that the best thing they could do was to go away.' Others, however, are naturally skilled. In the eighteenth century, William

217

Pitt was asked by a Frenchmen why the dissolute Charles James Fox wielded such influence. Pitt's response was that the answer lay in Fox's powers as an orator. The Frenchman had not experienced them: 'You have not been under the wand of the magician.'

Skill apart, there is also technique. The poet Charles Churchill suggested that 'Adepts in the speaking trade, Keep a cough by them ready made.' And in 2007, presidential hopeful Barack Obama explained how he differentiated between large and small audiences: 'I use a different style if I'm speaking to a big crowd; I can gin up folks pretty well. But when I'm in these town hall settings, my job is not to throw them a lot of red meat. I want to give them a sense of my thought processes.'

Solon compared the people unto the sea, and orators to the winds: for that the sea would be calm and quiet, if the winds did not trouble it.
– FRANCIS BACON

Grasp the subject; the words will follow.
– CATO THE ELDER

Amplification is the vice of the modern orator ... Speeches measured by the hour die with the hour.
– THOMAS JEFFERSON

The object of oratory alone is not truth, but persuasion.
– LORD MACAULAY

**A speech is poetry: cadence, rhythm, imagery, sweep ...
and reminds us that words, like children, have the power
to make dance the dullest beanbag of a heart.**
– PEGGY NOONAN

Be sincere; be brief; be seated.
– FRANKLIN ROOSEVELT

* * *

Sport

see also Competition, Leisure

Traditionally, sport has often been associated with character-building challenges and fair play, the world of Henry New-bolt's exhortation, 'Play up! play up! and play the game!' In Thomas Hughes's *Tom Brown's Schooldays*, Tom's own view of cricket was that 'It's more than a game. It's an institution.' (His friend Arthur replied resoundingly that 'It is the birth-right of British boys old and young, as *habeas corpus* and trial by jury are of British men.') A sporting image was even borrowed for the distinctly unsporting world of espionage. In Kipling's story, Kim, outwitting Russian agents on the North-West frontier, saw himself and his associates as 'playing the Great Game'. The Duke of Wellington is said to have given it as his view that 'The battle of Waterloo was won on the playing-fields of Eton.' (In the twentieth century, George Orwell gave a qualified assent to this: 'Probably the battle of Waterloo was won on the playing-fields of Eton, but the opening battles of all subsequent wars have been lost there.')

Some people have taken a distinctly relaxed approach to sport. The nineteenth-century writer and wit Douglas Jerrold once said, 'The only athletic sport I ever mastered was backgammon.' William Temple, headmaster of Repton in the 1930s, is said to have told parents, 'Personally, I have always looked on cricket as organized loafing.' In our own time, P. J. O'Rourke has commented, 'The sport of skiing consists of wearing three thousand dollars' worth of clothes and equipment and driving two hundred miles in order to stand round at a bar and get drunk.'

For those fully engaged in their particular sport, however, things are different. The American critic Rita Mae Brown thought that 'Sport strips away personality, letting the white bone of character shine through.' Although the phenomenally successful tennis player Martina Navratilova has put sporting success in a wider context: 'The moment of victory is much too short to live for that and nothing else.'

Sport is something that does not matter, but is performed as if it did. In that contradiction lies its beauty.
– SIMON BARNES

A game is exactly what is made of it by the character of the men playing it.
– NEVILLE CARDUS

The thing about sport, any sport, is that swearing is very much part of it.
– Jimmy Greaves

Winning is everything. The only ones who remember you when you come second are your wife and your dog.
– Damon Hill

There is no way sport is so important that it can be allowed to damage the rest of your life.
– Steve Ovett

Football? It's the beautiful game.
– Pelé

Some people think football is a matter of life and death. I don't like that attitude. I can assure them it is much more serious than that.
– Bill Shankly

The sports section records man's accomplishments; the front page has nothing but man's failures.
– Earl Warren
(the US Chief Justice on why he turned first to the sports
 section of a newspaper)

The least thing upset him on the links. He missed short putts because of the uproar of the butterflies in the adjoining meadows.
– P. G. Wodehouse

* * *

Success

see also Achievement, Determination

The American writer Gore Vidal admitted that 'It is not enough to succeed. Others must fail', and a good many comments on success in life carry a strong sense of what it is like *not* to succeed. Despite Oscar Wilde's view that 'Success is a science', there is no magic formula. Alan Jay Lerner said ruefully, 'You write a hit the same way you write a flop.' And as the actress Rosalind Russell pointed out, 'Success is a public affair. Failure is a private funeral.'

Self-belief may help (Mark Twain recommended a blend of 'ignorance and confidence'). It can also be important to convince others. In the seventeenth century, La Rochefoucauld noted that 'To succeed in this world we do all we can to appear successful.' Determination is probably essential too, although W. C. Fields sounded a cautionary note: 'If at first you don't succeed, try, try again. Then quit. No use being a damn fool about it.' (Homer Simpson's view was that 'Trying is the first step towards failure.') But in the end, of course, success is never predictable. Max Bialystock in Mel Brooks's *The Producers*, confronted by a hit instead of the surefire failure which his finances demanded, was left demanding sadly, 'Where did we go right?'

Get up early, work late – and strike oil.
– JOHN PAUL GETTY

Your success story is a bigger story than whatever you're trying to say on stage.
– MONTESQUIEU

To follow, without halt, one aim: There's the secret of success.
– ANNA PAVLOVA

All you need in this life is ignorance and confidence; then success is sure.
– MARK TWAIN

They can because they think they can.
– VIRGIL

Success is a science; if you have the conditions, you get the result.
– OSCAR WILDE

* * *

Teaching

see also **Education**

George Bernard Shaw's well-known dictum 'He who can, does. He who cannot, teaches' might be taken to imply that teaching is an easy as well as natural second option, but enough has been said and written about the profession to make it clear that this would be a facile assumption. In 1818, for example, the young Thomas Carlyle came to the conclusion that 'It were better to perish than to continue schoolmastering.' A century later, Sellar and Yeatman warned that 'For every person wishing to teach there are thirty not wanting to be taught.' In the 1950s, Vladimir Nabokov suggested that a more relaxed style of instruction would not necessarily bring relief. 'Discussion in class ... means letting twenty young blockheads and two cocky neurotics discuss something that neither they nor their teacher know.'

These negative views, fortunately, can be countered by voices through the ages. In Chaucer's *Canterbury Tales*, the 'clerk of Oxenford' is a young scholar of whom it is said that 'Gladly wolde he lerne and gladly teche.' Teaching is seen as being both of value to others, and to yourself. The American historian and memoirist Henry Adams wrote in 1907 that 'A teacher affects eternity; he can never tell where his influence stops.' And at the end of the twentieth century, the teacher and astronaut Christa McAuliffe, one of the seven people who died in the Challenger disaster, proudly adopted the motto 'I touch the future. I teach.'

The best teacher is one who suggests rather than dogmatizes, and inspires his listener with the wish to teach himself.
– EDWARD BULWER-LYTTON

Headmasters have powers at their disposal with which Prime Ministers have never been invested.
– WINSTON CHURCHILL

The whole art of teaching is only the art of awakening the natural curiosity of young minds for the purpose of satisfying it afterwards.
– ANATOLE FRANCE

To teach is to learn twice over.
– JOSEPH JOUBERT

The greatest sign of success for a teacher ... is to be able to say, "The children are now working as if I did not exist."
– MARIA MONTESSORI

Let such teach others who themselves excel.
– ALEXANDER POPE

* * *

Technology

see also Cyberspace, Innovation, Progress, Science

In *Gulliver's Travels*, Jonathan Swift gave a vivid picture of a doomed attempt to develop technology. Lemuel Gulliver has arrived in the city of Lagada, where the first man he sees is a would-be inventor. 'He has been eight years upon a project for extracting sunbeams out of cucumbers, which were to be put in phials hermetically sealed, and let out to warm the air in inclement summers.' Lemuel, unable to share the inventor's optimism that in eight years more his device would be successful, gives him 'a small present' to defray the high price of cucumbers.

Sunbeams from cucumbers may be taken as a type of technology that is bound to fail (while incurring costs), but most anxieties about technology relate not to failure but to success. The perception here is that technological development somehow separates us from an essential understanding of the world. In the nineteenth century, Ralph Waldo Emerson wrote, 'The machine unmakes the man. Now that the machine is so perfect, the engineer is nobody.'

The German writer Rainer Maria Rilke thought in the 1920s that 'The machine threatens all achievement.' And C. P. Snow was quoted in 1971 as saying, 'Technology ... is a queer thing. It brings you great gifts with one hand, and it stabs you in the back with the other.' The same note of caution is found in the fictional world of Harry Potter, created by J. K. Rowling, where Mr Weasley warned his son Ron, 'Never trust anything that can think for itself if you can't see where it keeps its brain.'

Perhaps the essential fear is of a Frankenstein's monster: something that has been developed but which can no longer be controlled. It is reassuring in that context to turn to the comment of the American physicist Richard Feynman: 'For a successful technology, reality must take precedence over public relations, for Nature cannot be fooled.'

Any sufficiently advanced technology is
indistinguishable from magic.
– ARTHUR C. CLARKE

No one needs a word processor if he has an efficient
secretary.
– ROBERTSON DAVIES

Technology is the knack of so arranging the world that
we do not experience it.
– MAX FRISCH

Paper is no longer a big part of my day.
– BILL GATES

Only a real lazybones can produce labour-saving
inventions.
– GÜNTER GRASS

It's not just what it looks like and feels like. Design is
how it works.
– STEVE JOBS

The machine does not isolate man from the great
problems of nature, but plunges him more deeply into
them.
– ANTOINE DE SAINT-EXUPÉRY

* * *

Thought

see also Ideas, Intelligence, Memory

A number of comments attest the importance, and power, of thought. The Roman emperor and Stoic philosopher Marcus Aurelius said that 'The universe is change; life is what thinking makes of it.' In Shakespeare's play, Hamlet told Rosencrantz and Guildenstern, 'There is nothing either good or bad, but thinking makes it so.' The philosopher Descartes is remembered for his assertion '*Cogito, ergo sum*', 'I think, therefore I am.'

Ralph Waldo Emerson highlighted the capacity of thought to disturb settled ways: 'Beware when the great God lets loose a thinker on the planet. Then all things are at risk.' In the late twentieth century, Dr Seuss evoked the possibility of unfettered imagination in a more encouraging way: 'Think left and think right and think low and think high. Oh, the thinks you can think up if only you try.'

Thought requires effort. 'There's nothing of so infinite vexation As man's own thoughts,' wrote John Webster in his 1612 play *The White Devil*. 'Thinking to me is the greatest fatigue in the world,' said Lord Foppington in Vanbrugh's *The Relapse*. In the twentieth century Bertrand Russell commented, 'Many people would sooner die than think. In fact they do.' The newspaper proprietor Lord Thomson said shortly, 'Thinking is work.'

I prefer thought to action, ideas to events, meditation to movement.
– Honoré de Balzac

Never express yourself more clearly than you think.
– Niels Bohr

Learning without thought is labour lost; thought without learning is perilous.
– Confucius

There's this thing called being so open-minded your brains drop out.
– Richard Dawkins

Everything worth thinking has already been thought, our concern must only be to try to think it through again.
– Goethe

When the facts change, I change my mind. What do you do?
– John Maynard Keynes

Great thoughts come from the heart.
– Marquis de Vauvenargues

*   *   *

Time

see also **Future, Past, Present, Punctuality**

Traditional representations of Old Father Time show him as carrying an hour-glass and a scythe, and some of our best known verbal images are similarly threatening. Andrew Marvell, appealing to his 'coy mistress', wrote, 'But at my back I always hear Time's winged chariot hurrying near.' The French romantic composer Hector Berlioz is said to have commented, 'Time is a great teacher, but unfortunately it kills all its pupils.' A character in Yeats's 1892 play *The Countess Cathleen* lamented, 'The years like great black oxen tread the world ... And I am broken by their passing feet.' In Noël Coward's *Blithe Spirit*, the medium Madame Arcati declaimed, 'Time is the reef on which our frail mystic ships are wrecked.'

Even if time is not seen as a personal aggressor, we should be aware of its inexorable progress. Lord Chesterfield told his son, 'I recommend to you to take care of minutes; for hours will take care of themselves.' In the nineteenth century the American educationist Horace Mann developed an elaborate image about the dangers of wasting such a precious commodity: 'Lost, yesterday, somewhere between Sunrise and Sunset, two golden hours, each set with sixty diamond minutes. No reward is offered, for they are gone for ever.' It is something of a relief, after this portentous piece of advice, to find J. M. Barrie as Rector of St Andrews taking a very different approach: 'You must have been warned against letting

the golden hours slip by. Yes, but some of them are golden
only because we let them slip.'

**He that will not apply new remedies, must expect new
evils; for time is the greatest innovator.**
– Francis Bacon

Yet while there is time, there is the certainty of return.
– Gavin Maxwell

**A good holiday is one spent among people whose notions
of time are vaguer than yours.**
– J. B. Priestley

**Time is the coin of our lives. We must take care how we
spend it.**
– Carl Sandburg

Time is but the stream I go a-fishing in.
– Henry David Thoreau

Though I am never in haste, I am never in a hurry.
– John Wesley

* * *

Trains

see also Travel

From the nineteenth century onwards, railways have been part of the literary scene. Lord Tennyson's opening line for his poem 'Godiva' ran, 'I waited for the train at Coventry.' In 1890, the Scottish doggerel poet William McGonagall marked the Tay Bridge Disaster with is verses on the collapse of the 'Beautiful railway bridge of the silv'ry Tay'. The novelist Anthony Trollope recorded the way in which railway travel became part of his creative life: 'I found that I passed in railway carriages very many hours of my existence ... I made for myself a little tablet, and found that I could write as quickly in a railway carriage as I could at my desk.'

Railway references can encapsulate a particular place or period. Rupert Brooke, in 1912 Berlin, was touched by memories of Grantchester and honey for tea: 'God! I will pack and take a train, And get me to England once again.' John Betjeman evoked his lost 'rural Middlesex' in a poem beginning, 'Gaily into Ruislip Gardens, runs the red electric train.' W. H. Auden's 'This is the Night Mail crossing the Border, Bringing the cheque and the postal order' is a reminder of pre-email days in which communications depended on the train. And a railway world dating from the 1950s has given a utilitarian phrase to the language. As the Fat Controller told Thomas the Tank Engine, he had a 'lot to learn about trucks'. However, once this knowledge had been acquired (by 'pushing them about here for a few weeks'), Thomas would know as much about them as his fellow engine, Edward: 'Then you'll be a Really Useful Engine.'

My policy is to be able to take a ticket at Victoria Station and go anywhere I damn well please.
– ERNEST BEVIN
(on foreign policy)

The only way to be sure of catching a train is to miss the one before it.
– G. K. CHESTERTON

If God had intended us to fly, he'd never have given us railways.
– MICHAEL FLANDERS AND DONALD SWANN

Railway termini ... are our gates to the glorious and the unknown. Through them we pass out into adventure and sunshine, to them, alas! we return.
– E. M. FORSTER

Sir, Saturday morning, although recurring at regular and well-foreseen intervals, always seems to take this railway by surprise.
– W. S. GILBERT
(complaining about the Metropolitan line)

233

I never travel without my diary. One should always have something sensational to read in the train.
– OSCAR WILDE

She had a penetrating sort of laugh. Rather like a train going into a tunnel.
– P. G. WODEHOUSE

* * *

Travel

see also Trains

The word 'travel' can cover a range of journeys, from tourist trips to exploration. For some people, the pleasure lies in the end of the journey, but for others, the journeying is an end in itself. As Robert Louis Stevenson wrote, 'I travel not to go anywhere, but to go. The great affair is to move.'

In the twentieth century, Hilaire Belloc developed this idea with an important distinction: 'I have wandered all my life, and I have also travelled; the difference between the two being this, that we wander for distraction, but we travel for fulfilment.' His view that travel needs some kind of focus to be fruitful resonates with the words of Marcel Proust: 'The only true voyage of discovery, the only fountain of Eternal Youth, would be not to visit strange lands but to possess other eyes to behold the universe.' Or, as the American novelist James A. Michener put it more prosaically, 'If you reject the food, ignore the customs, fear the religion, and avoid the people, you might better stay home.'

Those who have experienced and enjoyed what the eighteenth-century Scottish poet James Thomson called 'other lands beneath another sun' may wish to share what they have seen with others, but there are dangers here as well. The American writer Elizabeth Drew commented dryly, 'Too often travel, instead of broadening the mind, merely lengthens the conversation.' Vita Sackville-West, noting and explaining the same phenomenon, concluded that 'Travel is the most private of pleasures.' Nevertheless, the urge to communicate wonders is a natural one. According to one source, the last words of the Venetian traveller Marco Polo were, 'I have not told half of what I saw.'

The time to enjoy a European trip is about three weeks after unpacking.
– GEORGE ADE

My favourite thing is to go where I've never been.
– DIANE ARBUS

Polar exploration is at once the cleanest and most isolated way of having a bad time that has ever been described.
– APSLEY CHERRY-GARRARD

The beckoning counts, and not the clicking latch behind you.
– FREYA STARK

A journey is like marriage. The certain way to be wrong is to think you control it.
– JOHN STEINBECK

Not all those who wander are lost.
– J. R. R. TOLKIEN

* * *

The Weather

see also Nature

Comments about the weather recur in literature. Geoffrey Chaucer opened his *Canterbury Tales* with the words, 'Whan that Aprill with his shoures soote, The droghte of March hath perced to the roote.' The idea of April's 'showers sweet' ending the 'drought of March' is a pleasant one, and chimes in with the proverb 'April showers bring May flowers', but in the eighteenth century William Cowper had a rather bleaker vision. He referred to 'Our severest winter, commonly called the spring'.

Keats might write lyrically of September as the 'Season of mists, and mellow fruitfulness', but in the opinion of other writers the interval of good weather was brief indeed. Coleridge noted that 'Summer has set in with its usual severity', and Byron wrote of 'The English winter – ending in July To recommence in August'. And even if the sun did come out, it was not necessarily a satisfaction. As Jane Austen wrote

236

to her sister Cassandra in 1796, 'What dreadful hot weather we have! – It keeps one in a continual state of inelegance.' In the twentieth century, the critic Logan Pearsall Smith welcomed a break in good weather: 'Thank heavens, the sun has gone in, and I don't have to go out and enjoy it.'

While this might seem a little extreme, not everyone can achieve the resolute approach of John Ruskin. He was once asked by an undergraduate friend what was the use of painting in 'such very bad weather'. By his own account, 'I had no answer, except that ... for me, there was no bad weather, but only different kinds of pleasant weather.' He would however had been applauded by Stuart Rose, Chief Executive of Marks and Spencer, who in November 2006 when the company returned good results said comprehensively, 'Weather is for wimps.'

He who doesn't notice whether it is winter or summer is happy.
– Anton Chekhov

Those lazy, hazy, crazy days of summer.
– Nat King Cole

The weather forecast ... predicting every possible combination of weather for the next twenty-four hours without actually committing itself to anything specific.
– David Lodge

The best thing one can do,
When it is raining, is to let it rain.
– HENRY WADSWORTH LONGFELLOW

Let no man boast himself that he has got through the
perils of winter till at least the seventh of May.
– ANTHONY TROLLOPE

Everyone talks about the weather, but nobody does
anything about it.
– MARK TWAIN

* * *

Weddings

see also Marriage

According to the proverb, 'Happy is the bride the sun shines on.' The association of a wedding-day with good weather as well as general revelry was developed by the seventeenth-century poet Robert Herrick: 'I sing of brooks, of blossoms, birds and bowers: Of April, May, of June and July-flowers. I sing of maypoles, hock-carts, wassails, wakes, Of bride-grooms, brides, and of their bridal cakes.'

Bell-ringing is traditionally associated with a wedding, to the degree that Lord Byron used it as an image: 'All went merry as a marriage bell.' The American poet Edgar Allan Poe also saw wedding bells as notably joyous: 'Hear the mellow wedding bells, Golden bells! What a world of happiness their harmony foretells.'

Coleridge's Wedding Guest, fixed by the 'glittering eye' of the Ancient Mariner, had some reason to 'beat his breast', but those who manage to get to a wedding in time should be in suitable spirits. As the German poet and dramatist Friedrich Schiller warned, 'A gloomy guest suits not the marriage feast.' (It is reasonable to assume that few celebrations would follow the pattern of that of Gertrude and Claudius in Shakespeare's *Hamlet*, where, in the words of Gertrude's disapproving son, 'The funeral baked meats Did coldly furnish forth the marriage table.')

It may be tempting to think that elaborate preparations for ceremony and entertainment are required, but for those who need to consider their budget 'Daisy Bell', the popular song from the end of the nineteenth century, could offer reassurance: 'It won't be a stylish marriage, I can't afford a carriage, But you'll look sweet upon the seat Of a bicycle made for two!'

A princely marriage is the brilliant edition of a universal fact, and, as such, it rivets mankind.
– WALTER BAGEHOT

The bride hath paced into the hall,
Red as a rose is she.
– SAMUEL TAYLOR COLERIDGE

Get me to the church on time!
– ALAN JAY LERNER

Just say 'I do' whenever anyone asks you a question.
– RICHARD CURTIS
(from the film Four Weddings and a Funeral)

It has been said that a bride's attitude towards her betrothed can be summed up in three words: Aisle. Altar. Hymn.
– FRANK MUIR

A happy bridesmaid makes a happy bride.
– LORD TENNYSON

* * *

Women

see also Men

From 'the weaker vessel' of Tyndale's 1526 translation of the Bible, through William Alexander's 'The weaker sex, to piety more prone', it has never been difficult to find a traditional (male) view of women and the woman's role. Stereotypes may be found as easily in the seventeenth century, in Jean Racine's 'She wavers, she hesitates; in a word, she is a woman', as in the twentieth, in James Dyson's comment, 'I don't operate rationally. I think just like a woman.'

There are famous criticisms of women stepping outside their traditional sphere. In the sixteenth century John Knox fulminated against 'the monstrous regiment of women' as exemplified by the rule of Mary Tudor in England and the

Queen Regent Marie of Guise in Scotland. Two centuries later, Dr Johnson was concerned about the possibility of a woman preaching: 'Sir, a woman's preaching is like a dog's walking on his hinder legs. It is not done well; but you are surprised to find it done at all.'

Women can also puzzle and bewilder. Sigmund Freud is quoted as saying that 'The great question ... which I have not been able to answer, despite my thirty years of research into the feminine soul, is, 'What does a woman want?' One possible answer to that was given by Mary Wollstonecraft in the eighteenth century. In *A Vindication of the Rights of Women* (1792), she wrote, 'I do not wish them to have power over men; but over themselves.' Thackeray's adventuress Becky Sharp had a different approach, saying wistfully, 'I think I could be a good woman if I had five thousand a year.'

I am not a member of the weaker sex.
– LAUREN BACALL

I'm not denyin' the women are foolish: God Almighty made 'em to match the men.
– GEORGE ELIOT

So this gentleman said a girl with brains ought to do something with them besides think.
– ANITA LOOS

Well behaved women seldom make history.
– LAUREL THATCHER ULRICH

When women go wrong, men go right after them.
– MAE WEST

Whatever women do they must do twice as well as men to be thought half as good. Luckily this is not difficult.
– CHARLOTTE WHITTON

* * *

Work

see also Careers, Retirement

For some, work has been synonymous with oppressive drudgery. Philip Larkin asked, 'Why should I let the toad work Squat on my life?' Bertrand Russell warned against over-absorption in one's chosen line: 'One of the symptoms of approaching nervous breakdown is the belief that one's work is terribly important. If I were a medical man, I should prescribe a holiday to any patient who considered his work important.'

There are, however, many for whom work is seen in a very different light. 'Blessed is he who has found his work; let him ask no other blessedness,' wrote Thomas Carlyle. It was Theodore Roosevelt's view that 'No man needs sympathy because he has to work ... Far and away the best prize that life offers is the chance to work hard at work worth doing.' (He would presumably have deplored the approach of George, one of Jerome K. Jerome's Three Men in a Boat, to his chosen employment: 'George goes to sleep at a bank from ten to four each day, except Saturdays, when they wake him up and put him outside.') The approach of the New Zealand writer Frank Sargeson would have been more to his taste. Sargeson reputedly kept a notice pinned to his front door to discourage callers: 'Frank Sargeson works in the morning. Do you?'

That was were certainty lay, in everyday work ... The essential thing was to do one's job well.
– ALBERT CAMUS

Perfect freedom is reserved for the man who lives by his own work and in that work does what he wants to do.
– R. G. COLLINGWOOD

Work is much more fun than fun.
– NOËL COWARD

One never notices what has been done; one can only see what remains to be done.
– MARIE CURIE

The work never is done while the power to work remains.
– OLIVER WENDELL HOLMES, JR

Relationships end, men fail, but your work will never let you down.
– ZANDRA RHODES

* * *

Writing

see also **Publishing, Reading**

Sir Philip Sidney has left an affecting picture of a frustrated writer, unable to find the right words, biting his 'tongue and pen' until inspiration came: '"Fool," said my muse to me, "look in thy heart and write."'

A writer needs to arrest the attention of the reader, and in Sheridan's *The Critic*, Puff's account of the opening of his play about the Spanish Armada took account of this: 'I open with a clock striking, to beget an awful attention in the audience: it also marks the time, which is four o'clock in the morning, and saves a description of the rising sun, and a great deal about gilding the eastern hemisphere.' In the nineteenth century Charles Reade had a recipe for a successful novel: 'Make 'em laugh; make 'em cry; make 'em wait.'

There are differing views as to why someone becomes a writer. Dr Johnson said, with his usual decision, 'No man but a blockhead ever wrote except for money.' On the other hand, it may be an inborn faculty; Richard Steele wrote that he had 'often thought that a storyteller is born, as well as a poet'. In the twentieth century, Julie Burchill combined elements of both these comments: 'Writing is more than anything a compulsion, like some people wash their hands thirty times a day for fear of awful consequences if they do not. It pays a whole lot better than this type of compulsion, but it is no more heroic.'

For a long time now I have tried simply to write the best I can. Sometimes I have good luck and write better than I can.
– ERNEST HEMINGWAY

Writing is like getting married. One should never commit oneself until one is amazed at one's luck.
– IRIS MURDOCH

I care not who knows it – I write for the general amusement.
– SIR WALTER SCOTT

Writing is easy. I just open a vein and bleed.
– RED SMITH

You can only write about what bites you.
– TOM STOPPARD

Three hours a day will produce as much as a man ought to write.
– ANTHONY TROLLOPE

* * *

Youth

see also Age, Middle Age

'Youth's the season made for joys,' wrote John Gay in *The Beggar's Opera* (1728), and youth is indeed often seen as a carefree time. Wordsworth, looking back on the late eighteenth century and Revolutionary France, wrote, 'Bliss was it in that dawn to be alive, But to be young was very heaven.' It will not last – as Feste sings in *Twelfth Night*, 'Then come kiss me, sweet and twenty; Youth's a stuff will not endure' – but it is delightful while it does. We may be advised to make the most of it. In the nineteenth century, Robert Louis Stevenson wrote, 'Youth is the time to go flashing from one end of the world to the other both in mind and body; to try the manners of different nations; to hear the chimes at midnight.' The Canadian writer Margaret Atwood, however, was more sceptical: 'I've never understood why people consider youth a time of freedom and joy. It's probably because they have forgotten their own.'

Youth may indicate inexperience. Cleopatra, looking back at her younger self, referred to 'My salad days, When I was green in judgement'. William Pitt, later Lord Chatham, once told the House of Commons, 'The atrocious crime of being a young man … I shall neither attempt to palliate or deny.' But whatever their levels of knowledge, the young may have an important function. According to George Bernard Shaw, their role in respect of the old is to 'shock them and keep them up to date'.

246

Youth would be an ideal state if it came a little later in life.
– HERBERT ASQUITH

Young men are fitter to invent than to judge; fitter for execution than for counsel, and fitter for new projects than for settled business.
– FRANCIS BACON

Youth is something very new; twenty years ago no one mentioned it.
– COCO CHANEL

The young always have the same problem – how to rebel and conform at the same time. They have now solved this by defying their parents and copying one another.
– QUENTIN CRISP

Fortune, like a woman, is friendly to the young, because they show her less respect, they are more daring and command her with audacity.
– MACHIAVELLI

Youth cannot know how age thinks and feels. But old men are guilty if they forget what it was to be young.
– J. K. ROWLING

*   *   *

Thematic Index

A

automobiles *see* CARS
autumn *see* WEATHER

B

BABIES *see also* BIRTH, CHILDREN, FAMILIES, PARENTS
beer *see* DRINK
BELIEF *see also* GOD
BEREAVEMENT *see also* DEATH, GRIEF
BIRTH *see also* BABIES, BIRTHDAYS
BIRTHDAYS *see also* AGE, BIRTH
BOATS *see also* ARMED FORCES, TRAVEL
body, the *see* APPEARANCE
books *see* READING, WEATHER, WRITING
BOREDOM *see also* PATIENCE, RETIREMENT
brandy *see* DRINK
bravery *see* COURAGE
BUREAUCRACY *see also* BUSINESS, MANAGEMENT, MEETINGS
BUSINESS *see also* BUREAUCRACY, MANAGEMENT,
   OPPORTUNITY, SUCCESS
buying *see* BUSINESS

C

CAREERS *see also* ACHIEVEMENT, AMBITION, BUSINESS,
   MANAGEMENT
CARS *see also* PROGRESS, TRAVEL

D

DEATH *see also* BEREAVEMENT, GRIEF, LOVE
DEPARTURE *see also* ARRIVAL, RETIREMENT
DETERMINATION *see also* COURAGE, SUCCESS
diamond *see* JEWELLERY
DIETS *see also* FOOD
DOGS *see also* CATS
drawing *see* ART
dress *see* FASHION
DRINK *see also* FOOD
driving *see* CARS
dullness *see* BOREDOM

E

EDUCATION *see also* EXAMINATIONS, TEACHING
effort *see* ACHIEVEMENT
email *see* CYBERSPACE
emerald *see* JEWELLERY
enquiry *see* CURIOSITY
EXAMINATIONS *see also* EDUCATION
experience *see* AGE
exploration *see* TRAVEL

F

G

government *see* POLITICS
grammar *see* LANGUAGE
green issues *see* NATURE
GRIEF *see also* BEREAVEMENT, DEATH, HAPPINESS
guests *see* HOSPITALITY

H

HAPPINESS *see also* GRIEF
HEALTH *see also* DIETS
holiday *see* LEISURE
Hollywood *see* FILM
HOME *see also* GARDENS, HOSPITALITY
HONESTY
HOPE
HORSES *see also* LEISURE, SPORT
HOSPITALITY *see also* FOOD, HOME
hosts *see* HOSPITALITY
housework *see* HOME
HUMOUR

I

IDEAS *see also* INNOVATION, INTELLIGENCE, THOUGHT
IDLENESS *see also* LEISURE, WORK
imagination *see* IDEAS

INNOVATION *see also* BUSINESS, CHANGE, IDEAS, PROGRESS
INTELLIGENCE *see also* IDEAS, THOUGHT

J

JEWELLERY *see also* APPEARANCE
jokes *see* HUMOUR
JOURNALISM *see also* WRITING
journeys *see* TRAVEL
joy *see* HAPPINESS
justice *see* LAW

K

kittens *see* CATS
KNOWLEDGE *see also* EDUCATION, SCIENCE

L

LANGUAGE *see also* CONVERSATION, WRITING
laughter *see* HUMOUR
LAW
learning *see* EDUCATION, KNOWLEDGE
leaving *see* DEPARTURE
LEISURE *see also* IDLENESS, WORK

letters *see* COMMUNICATION
LIFE *see also* CAREER, DEATH
literature *see* READING, WRITING
looks *see* APPEARANCE
loss *see* BEREAVEMENT
LOVE *see also* FRIENDSHIP, MARRIAGE
LUCK *see also* SUCCESS

M

MANAGEMENT *see also* BUREACRACY, BUSINESS, CAREERS
MARRIAGE *see also* LOVE, WEDDINGS
maturity *see* AGE
meaning *see* COMMUNICATION
meeting *see* ARRIVAL
MEETINGS *see also* BUREAUCRACY
MEMORY *see also* CELEBRITY, PAST
MEN *see also* WOMEN
MIDDLE AGE *see also* AGE, YOUTH
mind *see* THOUGHT
MONEY *see also* SUCCESS
MOTHERS *see also* BABIES, CHILDREN, FAMILIES, FATHERS,
  PARENTS
motors *see* CARS
mourning *see* BEREAVEMENT
MUSIC

N

NATURE *see also* GARDENS, PROGRESS, TECHNOLOGY
Navy *see* ARMED FORCES
news *see* JOURNALISM
newspapers *see* JOURNALISM

O

old age *see* AGE
OPPORTUNITY *see also* BUSINESS, HOPE, LUCK
optimism *see* HOPE

P

painting *see* ART
PARENTS *see also* BABIES, CHILDREN, FAMILIES, FATHERS,
   MOTHERS
parting *see* DEPARTURE
PAST *see also* FUTURE, MEMORY, PRESENT, TIME
PATIENCE *see also* HOPE, OPPORTUNITY
pearl *see* JEWELLERY
perseverance *see* DETERMINATION
pets *see* CATS, DOGS
pictures *see* ART
plants *see* GARDENS

POLITICS
ponies *see* HORSES
port *see* DRINK
pregnancy *see* BABIES
PRESENT *see also* FUTURE, PAST, TIME
presents *see* BIRTHDAYS
PROGRESS *see also* CHANGE, FUTURE, TECHNOLOGY
promotion *see* CAREERS
PUBLISHING *see also* READING, WRITING
PUNCTUALITY *see also* TIME
puppies *see* DOGS

Q

questions *see* CURIOSITY
QUOTATION *see also* LANGUAGE, SPEECHMAKING, WRITING

R

railways *see* TRAINS
READING *see also* PUBLISHING, WRITING
reform *see* CHANGE
RELATIONSHIPS *see also* FAMILIES, FRIENDSHIP, LOVE
religion *see* BELIEF
REPUTATION *see also* CELEBRITY, MEMORY
rest *see* LEISURE

S

SUCCESS *see also* ACHIEVEMENT, DETERMINATION

summer *see* WEATHER

T

talent *see* ACHIEVEMENT

TEACHING *see also* EDUCATION

TECHNOLOGY *see also* CYBERSPACE, INNOVATION,
   PROGRESS, SCIENCE

tennis *see* SPORT

theatre *see* ACTING

THOUGHT *see also* IDEAS, INTELLIGENCE, MEMORY

TIME *see also* FUTURE, PAST, PRESENT, PUNCTUALITY

TRAINS *see also* TRAVEL

TRAVEL *see also* TRAINS

truth *see* HONESTY

U

unemployment *see* IDLENESS

W

war *see* ARMED FORCES

wealth *see* MONEY

Index of Authors

A

Abbott, Diane (1953–), British politician **191**

Acheson, Dean (1893–1971), American politician **39**

Ackerley, J. R. (1896–1967), English writer **33**

Ackerman, Diane (1948–), American poet **155**

Acton, Eliza (1799–1859), English cookery writer **103**

Adams, Douglas (1952–2001), English writer **20, 74**

Adams, Franklin P. (1881–1960), American writer, poet and editor **171**

Adams, Henry (1838–1918), American historian and memoirist **146, 224**

Adams, John Quincy (1767–1848), American lawyer and diplomat, President of the United States **10, 127**

Adams, Scott (1957–), American cartoonist **61, 136, 182**

Addison, Joseph (1672–1719), English essayist, poet, and dramatist **58, 63, 65, 110, 131, 178**

Ade, George (1866–1944), American fabulist and dramatist **197, 235**

Adler, Polly (1900–62), American brothel keeper **154**

Aesop (6th century BC), Greek fabulist **111**

Aurelius, Marcus (121–180), Roman emperor and Stoic philosopher
  53, 228

Austen, Jane (1777–1817), English novelist **41, 54, 65, 66, 152, 156, 202, 215, 236**

Avery, Oswald Theodore (1877–1955), Canadian bacteriologist **182**

Awdry, W. (1911–97), English clergyman and writer of children's books, creator of Thomas the Tank Engine **232**

Ayer, A. J. (1910–89), English philosopher **197**

B

Bacall, Lauren (1924–), American film actress **134, 241**

Bacon, Francis (1561–1626), English philosopher, essayist and courtier **43, 75, 105, 125, 137, 145, 156, 182, 185, 196, 202, 215, 218, 231, 247**

Bagehot, Walter (1826–77), English economist and political philosopher **41, 133, 239**

Bailey, David (1938–), English photographer **94**

Bainbridge, Beryl (1934–), English novelist **167**

Baker, Russell (1925–), American writer **144**

Bakewell, Joan (1933–), English journalist and television presenter **44**

Baldwin, James (1924–87), American dramatist, poet and civil rights activist **114**

E

F

France, Anatole (1844–1924), French novelist, short-story writer and critic **70, 115, 225**

Franklin, Benjamin (1706–90), American statesman and scientist **81, 125, 192**

Franklin, Miles (1879–1954), Australian writer **170, 205**

Fraser, Malcolm (1930–), Australian statesman and Prime Minister **154**

Freud, Clement (1924–), British politician, broadcaster and writer **38**

Freud, Sigmund (1856–1939), Austrian neurologist, founder of psychoanalysis **30, 131, 241**

Friedan, Betty (1921–2006), American feminist leader and writer **2, 9**

Frisch, Max (1911–91), Swiss dramatist, writer and architect **227**

Frohman, Charles (1860–1915), American theatrical producer **76**

Frost, David (1939–), English broadcaster and writer **55**

Frost, Robert (1874–1963), American poet **32, 80, 121, 151**

Fry, Stephen (1957–), British comedian and writer **59, 134**

Frye, Northrop (1912–91), Canadian critic and academic **7, 203**

Fuller, Thomas (1607–61), English clergyman **58, 102**

G

Gabor, Zsa-Zsa (1919–), Hungarian born American actress **142, 164**

Galbraith, John Kenneth (1908–2006), Canadian-born American economist, diplomat and writer **165, 191**

I

Inge, William Ralph (1860–1954), English clergyman, writer and teacher **37, 54, 186**

Ingersoll, Robert Green (1833–99), American lawyer, orator and agnostic **126**

Ingrams, Richard (1937–), British journalist and satirist **151, 197**

Ingres, J. A. D. (1780–1867), French painter **23**

Irving, Washington (1783–1859), American writer and diplomat **52**

J

Jackson, Shirley (1916–65), American author **92**

Jackson, Thomas 'Stonewall' (1824–63), American soldier and Confederate general **68**

James, P. D. (1920–), English crime writer **185**

James, William (1842–1910), American psychologist and philosopher **118, 147, 197**

Jay, Douglas (1907–96), British politician and economist **38**

Jeans, James (1877–1946), English mathematician, physicist and astronomer **211**

Jefferson, Thomas (1743–1826), American statesman, President of the United States **6, 33, 56, 110, 145, 209, 218**

Jekyll, Gertrude (1843–1932), English artist and garden designer **110**

Jenkins, David (1925–), English clergyman and bishop **27**

K

L

M

N

O

P

Q

R

Roland, Madame (1754–93), French revolutionary and writer **83**

Rooney, Andy (1919–), American broadcaster and writer **83**

Rooney, Mickey (1920–), American film actor **117**

Roosevelt, Eleanor (1884–1962), American humanitarian, First Lady of the United States and wife of Franklin Delano Roosevelt **12, 31, 62, 72**

Roosevelt, Franklin Delano (1882–1945), American statesman, President of the United States **69, 81, 158, 219**

Roosevelt, Theodore (1858–1919), American statesman, President of the United States **62, 97, 242**

Rootes, Lord (1894–1964), English car manufacturer **47**

Rose, Stuart (1949–), British businessman **237**

Rosten, Leo (1908–97), Polish-born American social scientist, writer and humorist **24**

Roth, Eric (1945–), American screenwriter **57**

Rowland, Helen (1875–1950), American writer **121, 164, 183, 216**

Rowling, J. K. (1965–), English author, creator of Harry Potter **12, 31, 75, 226, 247**

Roy, Arundhati (1961–), Indian novelist **122**

Rubens, Paul Alfred (1875–1917), English songwriter **78**

Rubinstein, Helena (c.1872–1965), Polish-born American cosmetician and businesswoman **11, 15**

Runcie, Robert (1921–2000), English cleric, Archbishop of Canterbury **132**

T

U

V

W

Y

Young, Andrew (1932–), American politician and civil rights
campaigner **41**

Young, Edward (1683–1765), English poet, dramatist and
clergyman **198**

Youngman, Henny (1906–98), American comedian **87**

Z

Zappa, Frank (1940–93), American rock musician, songwriter and
record producer **145**

Index of Quotations

A

A baby is an inestimable blessing and bother. **26**

A baby is God's opinion that life should go on. **26**

A belief is not true because it is useful. **27**

A bore is a man who, when you ask him how he is, tells you. **36**

"Abroad", that large home of ruined reputations. **207**

Absence diminishes mediocre passions and increases great ones ... **79**

Absence from whom we love is worse than death. **77**

Absence of occupation is not rest. **208**

A canter is the cure for every evil. **128**

A carat figure large enough to make a turnip ... **142**

Accuracy, accuracy, accuracy. **145**

A celebrity is a person who works hard all his life to become ... **51**

A celebrity is one who is known to many persons he is glad ... **50**

... a coffin clapt in a canoe. **34**

A cold coming they had of it, at this time of the year ... **20**

A committee is a cul-de-sac down which ideas are lured ... **39**

A committee should consist of three men, two of whom are absent. **39**

A computer terminal is not some clunky old television with a ... **74**

A conference is a gathering of important people who singly ... **39, 165**

A critic is a man who knows the way but can't drive the car. **70**

Acting is a form of confusion. **5**

Actors don't pretend to be other people; they become themselves ... **5**

A cucumber should be well sliced, and dressed with pepper ... **103**

A cult of cheeriness and manliness, beer and cricket, briar ... **169**

Adepts in the speaking trade, Keep a cough by them ready made. **218**

A difference of taste in jokes is a great strain on the affections. **131**

A difficulty for every solution ... **40**

A diplomat is a person who can tell you to go to hell in such ... **62**

A dog teaches a boy fidelity, perseverance, and to turn around ... **84**

A door is what a dog is perpetually on the wrong side of. **84**

Ads are the cave art of the twentieth century. **8**

Advertisements contain the only truths to be relied on ... **6**

Advertising is a valuable economic factor because it is ... **8**

Advertising is the life of trade. **7**

Advertising is the most fun you can have with your clothes on. **7**

Advertising may be described as the science of arresting ... **6**

Advertising, with its judicious mixture of flattery and threats. **7**

Advice? I don't offer advice. Not my business. Your life is ... **9**

Advice is seldom welcome; and those who want it the most ... **9**

Advice is what we ask for when we already know the answer but ... **9**

Ae fond kiss, and then we sever! **77**

A film is a petrified fountain of thought. **99**

A fool ... is a man who never tried an experiment in his life. **138**

A memorandum is written not to inform the reader ... **39**

Americans are broad-minded people. **46**

Americans are fascinated by their own love of shopping ... **214**

A mother's role is to deliver children – obstetrically once, and ... **176**

A mother, who is really a mother, is never free. **176**

Amplification is the vice of the modern orator ... **218**

An actor's a guy who, if you ain't talking about him, ain't listening. **3**

An advertising agency is 85 per cent confusion and 15 per cent ... **7**

And malt does more than Milton can To justify God's words ... **85**

And of all axioms this shall win the prize ... **158**

And though home is a name, a word, it is a strong one; stronger ... **122**

And when did you last see your father? **96**

A new scientific truth does not triumph by convincing ... **212**

A newspaper consists of just the same number of words ... **143**

An idea isn't responsible for the people who believe in it. **135**

Animals are always loyal and love you, whereas with children ... **55**

Animals are such agreeable friends – they ask no questions ... **105**

Annual income twenty pounds, annual expenditure nineteen ... **173**

An original idea. That can't be too hard. The library must be ... **134**

... an unhappy Lottery winner. **158**

Any colour – so long as it's black. **45**

Any cook should be able to run the country. **160**

Any human being anywhere will blossom into a hundred ... **183**

Any man who hates dogs and babies can't be all bad. **24**

A star shines on the hour of our meeting. **21**

A successful artist would have no trouble being a successful ... **22**

As you grow older, you will discover that you have two hands ... **113**

A teacher affects eternity; he can never tell where his influence ... **224**

A theory can be proved by experiment; but no path leads from ... **212**

At one time I thought he wanted to be an actor ... **3**

At the age of six I wanted to be a cook. At seven I wanted ... **13**

Authors like cats because they are such quiet, lovable, wise ... **48**

A very merry Christmas, with roast beef in a violent perspiration ... **58**

Away with systems! **40**

A well-balanced person has a drink in each hand. **86**

A whale ship was my Yale College and my Harvard. **35**

A wise man will make more opportunities than he finds. **182**

A woman is only a woman, but a good cigar is a smoke! **216**

A word to the wise ain't necessary – it's the stupid ones who ... **9**

A world designed for automobiles instead of people would have ... **47**

B

... beautiful pea-green boat ... **34**

Beautiful railway bridge of the silv'ry Tay. **232**

Beauty is handed out as undemocratically as inherited peerages ... **16**

Beauty without vanity, strength without insolence, courage ... **84**

Be fearful when others are greedy and greedy only when others ... **42**

But screw your courage to the sticking place. **67**

... but the opening battles of all subsequent wars have been lost ... **220**

But the past, the beautiful past striped with sunshine, grey ... **186**

But you'll look sweet upon the seat Of a bicycle made for two! **239**

By and large, mothers and housewives are the only workers who ... **177**

By necessity, by proclivity – and by delight, we all quote. **200**

C

Caramels are just a fad, but chocolate is a permanent thing. **57**

Cats, no less liquid than their shadows ... **49**

Champagne, if you are seeking the truth, is better than ... **87**

Chance might be God's pseudonym when He does not want to ... **115**

Change imposed is change opposed. **52**

Change is inevitable. In a progressive country, change is constant. **53**

Change is not made without inconvenience, even from worse ... **52**

Character is like a tree and reputation like its shadow ... **208**

Children enjoy the present because they have neither a past ... **193**

Chocolate is not what it was to me. I was carried away ... **58**

Christmas, children, is not a date. It is a state of mind. **59**

Christmas to a child is the first terrible proof that to travel ... **59**

Claret is the liquor for boys; port for men; but he who aspires ... **85**

Classical quotation is the parole of the literary man. **201**

C-l-e-a-n, clean, verb active, to make bright, to scour. **88**

E

Every man, wherever he goes, is encompassed by a cloud ... **26**

Everyone complains of his memory; nobody of his judgement. **167**

Everyone is entitled to their own opinions, but not their own ... **124**

Everyone is in love with his own ideas. **135**

Everyone talks about the weather, but nobody does anything ... **238**

Every politician should have three hats handy at all times ... **192**

Every separation gives a foretaste of death, – and every reunion ... **79**

... everything about the wasp, except why. **72**

Everything comes to him who waits. **188**

Everything in life is somewhere else, and you get there in a ... **47**

Everything is funny as long as it is happening to someone else. **131**

Everything is on the move, nothing is constant. **53**

Everything I've ever said will be credited to Dorothy Parker ... **201**

Everything worth thinking has already been thought ... **229**

Every time I make an appointment, I make a hundred men ... **43**

Every time I paint a portrait I lose a friend. **22**

Examinations are formidable even to the best prepared ... **89**

Exams work because they're scary. **91**

F

Fame is not achieved by sitting on feather cushions or lying ... **2**

Fame is the spur that the clear spirit doth raise ... **50**

Fashion anticipates, and elegance is a state of mind. **95**

G

337

H

I

I ... chose my wife as she did her wedding gown ... **163**

I could have been a judge, but I never had the Latin. **90**

I could not, at any age, be really contented to take my place ... **12**

I did toy with the idea of doing a cook-book ... **197**

Idleness is only the refuge of weak minds, and the holiday of fools. **135**

I do like Christmas on the whole ... In its clumsy way, it does ... **59**

I do not believe in discarding human beings. **209**

I do not wish them to have power over men; but over themselves. **241**

I don't advise anyone to take it up as a business proposition ... **22**

I don't care what is written about me as long as it isn't true. **51**

I don't design clothes. I design dreams. **95**

I don't operate rationally. I think just like a woman. **240**

I dream for a living. **100**

I dress for the image. Not for myself, not for the public, not ... **95**

I drink for the thirst to come. **86**

If a fish is the movement of water embodied, given shape, then ... **49**

If a man does not make new acquaintance as he advances ... **106**

... if a man doesn't drive, there is something wrong with him. **46**

If any young men come for Mary or Kitty, send them in, for I am ... **152**

If, as you grow older, you feel you are also growing stupider ... **184**

If at first you don't succeed, try, try again. Then quit ... **222**

If Botticelli were alive today he'd be working for *Vogue*. **23**

If Cleopatra's nose had been shorter the whole face of the earth ... **15**

I feel about airplanes the way I feel about diets ... **82**

I feel no need for any other faith than my faith in human beings. **27**

I felt it shelter to speak to you. **205**

If everybody minded their own business, the world would ... **72**

If fishing is a religion, fly fishing is high church. **101**

If God had intended us to fly, he'd never have given us railways. **233**

If grass can grow through cement, love can find you at every ... **157**

If he had made any advances in those subjects, it was owing ... **189**

If I can't have too many truffles, I'll do without truffles. **82**

If I'd known I was gonna live this long, I'd have taken ... **120**

If I had been someone not very clever, I would have done an ... **197**

If I have seen further it is by standing on the shoulders of ... **212**

If I made Cinderella people would be looking for the body in ... **100**

I find myself surprised at how its realism actually unites morality ... **93**

If life had a second edition, how I would correct the proofs. **154**

If men were angels, no government would be necessary. **191**

If merely 'feeling good' could decide, drunkenness would be ... **118**

If music be the food of love, play on. **177**

If one cannot enjoy reading a book over and over again, there ... **204**

If one were to study all the laws, one would have absolutely no ... **150**

If only God would give me some clear sign! Like making a large ... **114**

I found that I passed in railway carriages very many hours of my ... **232**

If past history is all there was to the game, the richest people ... **187**

If the concept of God has any validity or any use, it can only be ... **114**

If the past cannot teach the present and the father cannot teach ... **187**

In his whole life man achieves nothing so great and so ... **149**

In Hollywood gratitude is Public Enemy Number One. **99**

In Italy for thirty years under the Borgias they had warfare ... **3**

In my conscience I believe the baggage loves me, for she never ... **157**

In my mind, there is nothing so illiberal and so ill-bred, as ... **132**

Innovation has nothing to do with how many R&D dollars ... **138**

Innovation is the specific instrument of entrepeneurship ... **138**

I no doubt deserved my enemies, but I don't believe I deserved ... **107**

In our family, there was no clear line between religion and ... **102**

In politics, what begins in fear usually ends in folly. **190**

In quoting of books, quote such authors as are usually read ... **200**

Intelligence is quickness to apprehend as distinct from ability ... **139**

In the defiance of fashion is the beginning of character. **94**

In the factory we make cosmetics. In the store we sell hope. **42**

In the future everyone will be world famous for fifteen minutes. **51**

In the morning I see sights, saunter from one museum to ... **213**

In the night of death, hope sees a star, and listening love ... **126**

In times of great stress, such as a four-day vacation, the thin ... **92**

In Vienna, even the Emperor did not dictate to my husband ... **161**

Invincibility depends on one's self, the enemy's vulnerability ... **64**

I often quote myself. It adds spice to my conversation. **202**

I only take a drink on two occasions: when I'm thirsty and when ... **86**

I open with a clock striking, to beget an awful attention in ... **244**

I prefer liberty to chains of diamonds. **143**

I think I could be a good woman if I had five thousand a year. **241**

I think I owe my success (as the millionaires say) to having ... **9**

I think it takes the soul out of food ... **103**

I think the answer lies somewhere between conversation and ... **57**

I think the British have the distinction above all other nations ... **137**

I think, therefore I am. **228**

I think there is a world market for about five computers. **73**

It is a good deed to forget a poor joke. **132**

It is a good thing for an uneducated man to read books ... **201**

It is a law of the natural universe that no being can exist ... **180**

It is a pleasant thing to reflect upon ... **25**

It is a truth universally acknowledged ... **215**

It is because we put up with bad things that hotel-keepers ... **188**

It is better to be born lucky than rich. **159**

It is better to die young than to outlive all one loved ... **76**

It is better to give than to lend, and it costs about the same. **112**

It is better to have loafed and lost than never to have loafed at all. **136**

It is better to travel hopefully than to arrive. **125**

It is by attempting to reach the top at a single leap that so ... **14**

It is difficult to get a man to understand something when his ... **42**

It is far easier to write ten passably effective sonnets ... **6**

It is impossible to enjoy idling thoroughly unless ... **135**

It is in our idleness, in our dreams, that the submerged truth ... **137**

It is not a bad thing that children should occasionally, and ... **185**

J

K

L

Life shrinks or expands in proportion to one's courage. **68**

Life was meant to be lived. Curiosity must be kept alive. **72**

Life wouldn't be worth living if I worried over the future as ... **109**

Like all the best families, we have our share of eccentricities ... **92**

... Lillian, you should have stayed a virgin ... **175**

[London's parks are] the lungs of London. **180**

Look, he's winding up the watch of his wit, By and by it will strike. **139**

Lord I disbelieve – help thou my unbelief. **26**

Lord Salisbury motored ... **46**

Lost, yesterday, somewhere between Sunrise and Sunset ... **230**

Lots of meat, drink and cigarettes and not giving in to things. **119**

Love and scandal are the best sweeteners of tea. **65**

Love, having no geography, knows no boundaries. **157**

Love is like the measles; we all have to go through it. **157**

Love is not looking into one another's eyes but looking together ... **158**

Love makes the world go round. **156**

Lovers' quarrels are the renewal of love. **158**

Love springs from blindness, friendship from knowledge. **105**

Loving a baby or child is a circular business, a kind of feedback ... **25**

... loving longest, when existence or when hope is gone. **156**

M

Make 'em laugh; make 'em cry; make 'em wait. **244**

Mama exhorted her children at every opportunity ... **176**

Management is nothing more than motivating other people. **162**

Man invented language in order to satisfy his deep need ... **148**

Man is a gaming animal. He must always be trying to get ... **63**

Man is a knot, a web, a mesh into which relationships are tied. **206**

Man is by nature a political animal. **190**

Mankind is divisible into two great classes, hosts and guests. **129**

"Man wants but little here below" but likes that little good ... **188**

Man wants but little here below, nor wants that little long. **188**

Many ideas grow better when transplanted into another mind ... **133**

Many kids can tell you about drugs but do not know ... **104**

Many people would sooner die than think. In fact they do. **228**

Many's the long night I have dreamed of cheese – toasted mostly. **103**

Marriage is a framework to preserve friendship. It is valuable ... **164**

[Marriage is] a sort of friendship recognized by the police. **163**

[Marriage] resembles a pair of shears, so joined that they ... **163**

Massey won't be satisfied until somebody assassinates him. **4**

Meeting people unlike oneself does not enlarge one's outlook ... **20**

Meetings are indispensable when you don't want to do anything. **165**

Meetings ... are rather like cocktail parties. You don't want ... **166**

Men are clumsy, stupid creatures regarding little things, but ... **170**

Men are from Mars and women are from Venus. **169**

Men are often bad; babies never are. **24**

Men fear death as children fear to go in the dark ... **75**

Men generally believe what they wish. **27**

Men play the game; women know the score. **170**

Method, as Mrs More says, is the very hinge of business ... **198**

Middle age is when your age starts to show around the middle. **172**

Middle age is when you're faced with two temptations and you ... **172**

Miracles can be made, but only by sweating. **2**

Mirrors should reflect a little before throwing back images. **15**

Misquotations are the only quotations that are never misquoted. **202**

Money cannot buy happiness. **173**

Money speaks sense in a language all nations understand. **60**

Music is your own experience, your thoughts, your wisdom ... **179**

Music, the greatest good that mortals know. **178**

My boat is on the shore, And my bark is on the sea. **35**

My brain: it's my second favourite organ. **140**

My dear child, you must believe in God in spite of what ... **26**

My difficulty is trying to reconcile my gross habits with my ... **174**

My experience is what I agree to attend to. **147**

My experience of men is that when they begin to quote poetry ... **204**

My favourite thing is to go where I've never been. **235**

My films are therapy for my debilitating depression. **99**

My idea of exercise is a good, brisk sit. **120**

N

Never get a mime talking. He won't stop. **66**

Never give in, never never never ... except to convictions ... **80**

Never glad confident morning again! **186**

Never have children, only grandchildren. **55**

Never in the field of human conflict was so much owed ... **18**

Never in the history of fashion has so little material been raised ... **94**

Never submit to failure. **79**

Never take counsel of your fears. **68**

Never the time and the place, And the loved one all together. **199**

Never trust a husband too far or a bachelor too near ... **216**

Never trust anything that can think for itself if you can't see ... **226**

Never wear artistic jewellery; it ruins a woman's reputation. **142**

Never were abilities so much below mediocrity so well rewarded ... **127**

News is the first rough draft of history. **144**

No act of kindness, no matter how small, is ever wasted. **111**

No adversity is insurmountable. Regardless of the odds, I know ... **80**

No animal is so inexhaustible as an excited infant ... **25**

No blessed leisure for Love or Hope. **152**

Nobody ever talks of entrepeneurship as survival, but that's ... **139**

Nobody ever thought of putting [motherhood] on a moral ... **176**

Nobody knows anything. **98**

No brilliance is needed in the law. Nothing but common sense ... **151**

No coward soul is mine. **67**

No good deed goes unpunished. **111**

Nothing is ever done beautifully, which is done in rivalship. **64**

Nothing is illegal if one hundred businessmen decide to do it. **41**

Nothing is more dangerous than an idea, when you have ... **133**

Nothing is so delicate as the reputation of a woman ... **206**

Not many sounds in life, and I include all urban and rural ... **71**

Not many sounds in life ... exceed in interest a knock at the door. **71**

Not to be healthy ... is one of the few sins that modern society is ... **119**

Not to have hit once in so many trials, argues the most splendid ... **2**

Now Barabbas was a publisher. **197**

Now he belongs to the ages. **50**

Now the end, I take it, is all one, to live at more leisure ... **153**

O

O all ye Green Things upon the Earth, bless ye the Lord. **179**

O bliss! O poop-poop! O my! O my! **46**

Of all the means to ensure happiness throughout the whole ... **104**

Of all the qualities, indispensable in a cook, punctuality ... **199**

Of course I don't look busy. I did it right the first time. **136**

Oh, I have slipped the surly bonds of earth, And danced ... **19**

Oh, the comfort – the inexpressible comfort of feeling safe ... **205**

Old age ain't no place for sissies. **11**

Old age takes away from us what we have inherited and gives ... **12**

One advantage of being pregnant, you don't have to worry about ... **24**

On the keyboard of life, always keep one finger on the escape ... **182**

On the Road sold a trillion Levis and a million espresso ... **203**

Opportunity seldom knocks twice. **181**

Ordinary people are capable of doing extraordinary things. **2**

Our birthdays are feathers in the broad wing of time. **34**

Our birth is but a sleep and a forgetting. **32**

Our jets don't have bathrooms and I was driven to lessons ... **173**

Our motor car is our supreme form of privacy when away from ... **46**

Our severest winter, commonly called the spring. **236**

O, withered is the garland of the war, The soldier's pole is fallen! **17**

P

Painting is a blind man's profession. He paints not what he sees ... **22**

Paper is no longer a big part of my day. **227**

Parentage is a very important profession; but no test of fitness ... **183**

Parents are the last people on earth who ought to have children. **183**

Parents – especially step-parents – are sometimes a bit of a ... **184**

Parents learn a lot from their children about coping with life. **56, 185**

Parting is all we know of heaven, And all we need of hell. **77**

Parting is such sweet sorrow. **77**

Passion for fame; a passion that is the instinct of all great ... **51**

Patience. A minor form of despair, disguised as a virtue. **188**

Patience and time do more than force and rage. **188**

Politics is the art of human happiness. **191**

Politics is the art of the possible. **190**

Posterity – what you write for after being turned down ... **197**

Poverty is a lot like childbirth – you know it's going to hurt ... **31**

Power without responsibility – the prerogative of the harlot ... **144**

Probably the battle of Waterloo was won on the playing-fields ... **219**

Problems are only opportunities in work clothes. **183**

Procrastination is the thief of time. **198**

Progress might have been all right once, but it's gone on too ... **195**

Progress, therefore, is not an accident, but a necessity ... **194**

Promise, large promise, is the soul of an advertisement. **6**

Promotion cometh neither from the east, nor from the west ... **43**

Publish and be damned! **197**

Publishers are demons, there's no doubt about it. **197**

Punctuality is one of the cardinal business virtues ... **199**

Punctuality is the politeness of kings. **198**

... punctuality is the thief of time. **198**

Punctuality is the virtue of the bored. **199**

Pushing forty? She's clinging on to it for dear life. **11**

Q

Question and answer is not a civilized form of conversation. **65**

Quinquireme of Nineveh from distant Ophir ... **34**

S

Smile, it confuses people. **61**

Society drives people crazy with lust and calls it advertising. **7**

Solon compared the people unto the sea, and orators to ... **218**

Somebody's boring me. I think it's me. **36**

Some day some fellow will invent a way of concentrating ... **138**

Some enchanted evening, You may see a stranger ... **20**

Someone had blundered. **17**

Someone to tell it to is one of the fundamental needs of human ... **205**

Some people say, the glass is half empty, some say it is half full ... **125**

Some people think football is a matter of life and death ... **221**

Sometimes I wonder if men and women really suit each other ... **204**

Sometimes when I look at my children I say to myself ... **175**

So much of what we call management consists in making ... **162**

Sooner or later, I'm going to die, but I'm not going to retire. **210**

So this gentleman said a girl with brains ought to do something ... **241**

Speed, bonny boat, like a bird on the wing ... **34**

Sport is something that does not matter, but is performed as ... **220**

Sport strips away personality, letting the white bone ... **220**

Still Gertrude did not feel happy; but the usual panacea ... **213**

Strange to see how a good dinner and feasting reconciles ... **130**

Strike while the iron is hot. **181**

Strip the phoney tinsel off Hollywood and you'll find the real ... **98**

Study the past, if you would divine the future. **108**

Stung by the splendour of a sudden thought. **134**

T

The child is father of the man. **54**

The cinema has no boundaries. It's a ribbon of dream ... **99**

The courage to believe in nothing. **28**

The critical period in matrimony is breakfast-time. **164**

The desire for fame is the last thing to be put aside ... **51**

The desire of fame, And love of truth, and all that makes a man. **169**

The desire of knowledge, like the thirst of riches, increases ... **147**

The die is cast. **79**

The difference between good and bad cookery ... **103**

The difficulty lies, not in the new ideas, but in escaping from ... **138**

The discovery of a new dish does more for the happiness ... **102**

The dog is a Yes-animal, very popular with people who can't ... **85**

... the dreamers of dreams ... World losers, and world forsakers ... **177**

The effect of boredom on a large scale in history is underestimated. **37**

The English may not like music, but they absolutely love ... **177**

The English winter – ending in July To recommence in August. **236**

The essence of life is statistical improbability on a colossal scale. **154**

The follies which a man most regrets in his life are those which ... **183**

The frame and huge foundation of the earth Shaked like a coward. **30**

The French want to attack, the Americans want to bomb ... **165**

The fundamental defect of fathers is that they want ... **97**

The funeral baked meats Did coldly furnish forth ... **239**

The future doesn't belong to the fainthearted, it belongs to ... **69**

The future is already here – it's just unevenly distributed. **108**

Their meetings made December June. **21**

Theirs not to reason why. **17**

The joys of parents are secret, and so are their griefs and ... **185**

The last stages of life should not be seen as defeat, but rather ... **77**

The law is a ass – a idiot ... **150**

The law is the bedrock of a nation. It tells us who we are ... **151**

The Law of Triviality ... means that the time spent on any item ... **166**

The least thing upset him on the links. He missed short putts ... **221**

The length of a film should be directly related to the endurance ... **99**

The length of a meeting rises with the square of the number ... **166**

... the little ships of England brought the Army home. **35**

The living moment is everything. **193**

The Lord God planted a garden, eastward in Eden. **109**

The lot of critics is to be remembered by what they failed to ... **71**

The louder he talked of his honour, the faster we counted ... **130**

The love of gardening is a seed that once sown never dies. **110**

The love of money is the root of all evil. **173**

The machine does not isolate man from the great problems of ... **227**

The machine threatens all achievement. **226**

The machine unmakes the man. Now that the machine is ... **226**

The magi, as you know, were wise men ... **59**

... the magical influence which shopping possesses ... **213**

The manner of giving is worth more than the gift. **112**

The man who dies thus rich dies disgraced. **41**

374

U

Would God I had died for thee, O Absalom, my son! **28**

Would you convey my compliments to the purist ... **148**

Writing is easy. I just open a vein and bleed. **245**

Writing is like getting married. One should never commit ... **245**

Writing is more than anything a compulsion, like some people ... **244**

Y

Years ago, manhood was an opportunity for achievement ... **170**

Ye diners-out from whom we guard our spoons. **130**

Yes, Sir, you tossed and gored several persons. **64**

Yesterday is history, tomorrow's a mystery, but today is a gift ... **193**

Yes, Virginia, there is a Santa Claus. **58**

Yet while there is time, there is the certainty of return. **231**

You can always tell an old soldier by the inside of his holsters ... **19**

You can never go home again, but the truth is you can never ... **122**

You can only write about what bites you. **245**

You can run the office without a boss, but you can't run an ... **39**

You can say what you like about long dresses, but they cover ... **96**

You have got to be a Queen to get away with a hat like that. **95**

You have not been under the wand of the magician. **218**

You have to know the past to understand the present. **187**

You know, she speaks eighteen languages. And she can't ... **149**

You'll be a man, my son. **169**